Healthy You!

UNIT B
TAKING CARE OF YOURSELF

HARCOURT BRACE & COMPANY

Orlando Atlanta Austin Boston San Francisco Chicago Dallas New York
Toronto London

MW00885533

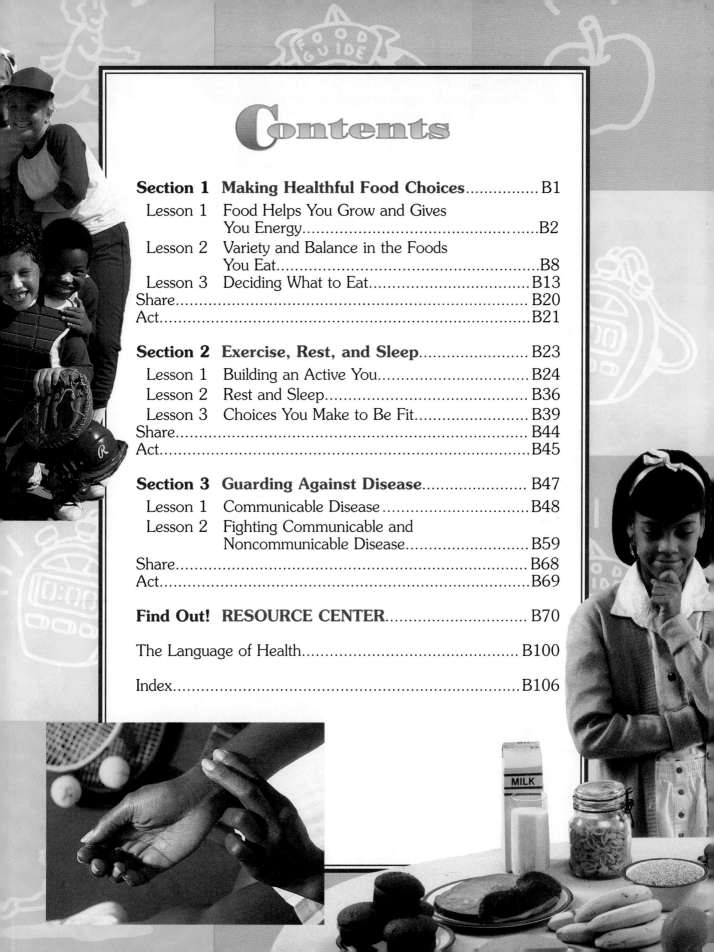

Contents

MAKING HEALTHFUL FOOD CHOICES

Some of the foods you like to eat may not always be the foods that your body needs. Eating the right foods will help you stay healthy. Your eating habits and food choices are important to your lifelong wellness.

ASK QUESTIONS

How does food help me grow and give me energy?
What can I do to have more healthful eating habits?
How can I learn to make healthful food choices?
What questions do *you* have?

Project

Develop a Food Display

With a Partner • Make a food display for other students in the school cafeteria or in a school display area. Arrange food pictures on paper plates and include information that explains why it is healthful. Add cutouts of healthful drinks. You can work on your food display as you gather information in the lessons in this section. Working on your display will help answer your questions.

1 Food Helps You Grow and Gives You Energy

Daniel's parents make sure that he gets all the foods he needs to stay healthy. Like Daniel, you need food for growth, for energy, and for helping your body work as it should. The parts of food that help your body grow and work and that give you energy are called *nutrients*.

How does food help me grow and give me energy?

- ▶ Refer to Unit A, pages A43–45, which discuss how your digestive system works.
- ▶ Look up food in a reference book, such as an encyclopedia.
- ▶ View the Health Video *International Food Fare* and do the suggested activities.
- ▶ Explore the activities and gather information from pages B2–7.

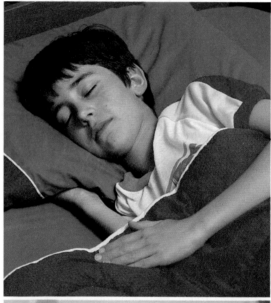

■ *You need sleep, exercise, and proper nutrients for good health. To get all the nutrients you need, you must eat many different kinds of foods.*

What Are the Energy Nutrients?

Three kinds of nutrients in foods give you energy. The energy nutrients are carbohydrates, fats, and proteins. You can get all the energy you need for good health by eating a variety of foods.

When Amanda drinks orange juice, she gets energy from the carbohydrates in it. **Carbohydrates** should be the nutrients that are your main source of energy each day. They give you energy to help you grow and be active. All fruits, vegetables, breads, and cereals are good sources of carbohydrates. Milk and other dairy foods also give you carbohydrates.

Fats are the nutrients that give you the greatest amount of energy. When you eat meat, eggs, and cheese, you get energy from the fats in these foods. Margarine, mayonnaise, and vegetable oil also have fats in them. Your body uses fats to provide the energy you need to be active.

Proteins are energy nutrients, too. But your body also uses proteins mainly to repair body cells and build new cells for growth. Because you are growing, you need to eat foods high in proteins every day. Meat, fish, eggs, nuts, and milk and other dairy foods all have a lot of the proteins you need.

Your body needs a variety of foods with carbohydrates, fats, and proteins. When you eat enough energy nutrients, your body can work at its best. When your body works at its best, you feel well and strong.

SCIENCE connection

NOTHING BUT THE FAT

With a Team • Rub a piece of celery on a section of a brown paper bag. Do the same with a small piece of ham. Let the bag dry. Then hold the bag up to the light. Food that contains fat will leave a greasy spot on the bag. Which food contains fat? Try some other foods.

■ *Energy nutrients in orange juice help Amanda grow and be active. But Amanda also needs fats and proteins.*

How Do Vitamins and Minerals Help You?

In addition to energy nutrients, your body needs vitamins and minerals. Vitamins and minerals are nutrients, but they do not give you energy. They help your body in other ways.

Vitamins. Each **vitamin** helps cause a specific reaction in the body. Vitamins with the letter names A and C, for example, work in different ways.

Vitamin A works with other nutrients to help you see well in dim light. Vitamin A also helps your bone cells grow and stay healthy. This vitamin helps keep your skin smooth and soft, too. Vitamin C works with other nutrients to help keep your gums and other body tissues healthy.

Look at the table called "Some Vitamins for Good Health." It lists some vitamins and the foods that are good sources of these vitamins. The table also tells how different kinds of vitamins help you.

SOME VITAMINS FOR GOOD HEALTH

Vitamin	Sources	What It Does
Vitamin A	carrots, milk, sweet potatoes	helps you see in dim light; helps keep bone cells and skin healthy
Vitamin B_1	breads, pork, whole-grain cereals	helps in digestion; helps nerves work
Vitamin B_2	meat, cheese, eggs	helps cells make energy; helps keep skin and hair healthy
Vitamin B_{12}	meat, fish	helps your nervous system
Vitamin C	orange juice, broccoli, strawberries, tomatoes	helps keep your gums and other tissues healthy
Vitamin D	saltwater fish, eggs, fortified milk	helps build strong bones and teeth

SOME MINERALS FOR GOOD HEALTH

Mineral	Sources	What It Does
Calcium	milk, cheese, yogurt	builds bones and teeth; helps blood to clot
Iron	dark green vegetables, peas, beans, meat	carries oxygen in the blood
Phosphorus	meat, peas, beans, whole grains	builds bones and teeth; helps your body use energy
Potassium	baked potatoes, lima beans, oranges	helps nerves and muscles work
Zinc	eggs, seafood, grains, nuts	helps nerves and muscles work

Minerals. Minerals are another kind of nutrient your body needs to help it grow and stay healthy. **Minerals** are nutrients used by the body in doing many things. They help the body work well. Two important minerals are calcium and iron.

The body uses calcium to help build bones and teeth and to make them strong. You have more calcium in your body than any other mineral. Many foods are good sources of calcium. Drinking milk and eating cheese or yogurt give you a lot of calcium.

Iron is a mineral that is in your blood. It helps carry oxygen in your red blood cells to all your other cells. Oxygen helps your cells use the energy nutrients they need. Dark green vegetables, peas, beans, whole grains, and meat, especially liver, have iron.

The table called "Some Minerals for Good Health" lists several minerals. It lists good sources for minerals in the foods you eat or drink. The table also has information on how your body uses each of the different minerals.

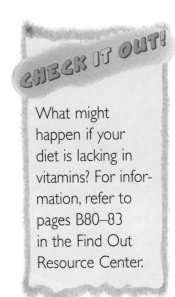

CHECK IT OUT!

What might happen if your diet is lacking in vitamins? For information, refer to pages B80–83 in the Find Out Resource Center.

How Do Water and Fiber Help Your Body?

Did you know that water is also a nutrient? Water is such an important nutrient that the body cannot live long without it. Most of your body is made of water. It is a part of every single cell. Water helps your body use other nutrients in food. It does this by breaking down the food and carrying the nutrients to where they are needed in the body.

When you drink milk or juice and even when you eat most foods, your body takes in water. Apples and many other fruits, for example, have a lot of water in them. To work well, your body needs at least 8 glasses (almost 2 liters) of water each day.

Fiber is also part of many foods you eat. **Fiber** is the "woody" substance in plants. It is needed by the body even though it cannot be digested. Fiber helps the

CHECK IT OUT!

What nutrients are in peanuts? Ask a librarian where to look for more information about peanuts.

■ *You can see the water in apples when they are crushed for juice. You can feel the fiber in apples by touching their skins.*

B6

body by helping move waste through the digestive system. Fiber helps keep this body system working as it should.

Many different foods have fiber. Almost all fruits and vegetables have fiber. Fiber is also in popcorn, whole grains, and cooked dry beans and peas. If you eat some of these foods daily, you will get the fiber your body needs for good health.

■ *Fiber is found in many foods, such as celery, beans, and popcorn. Break a celery stalk in two, and see the fiber.*

Project checkup

What information have you learned so far that you can add to your food display?

REFLECT

Information Check
1. Why do you need food?
2. How do vitamins and minerals differ?

Solving Problems
3. As part of breakfast, Amber wants to eat a whole-grain muffin with low-fat cream cheese. Are these good foods to eat for breakfast? Explain your answer.

Setting Goals
4. What goals can you set to make sure that your body gets the vitamins and minerals that it needs?

2 Variety and Balance in the Foods You Eat

How can you be sure you get the nutrients your body needs for good health? Dividing foods into food groups can help you plan your diet. Your **diet** is the combination of foods you eat each day.

What Are the Food Groups?

Terri has been asked to put the foods on the table into groups. How might she do this? Terri might group the foods by size or color. Or she might group the foods into those she likes and those she does not like. But there is another way to group foods. Terri can group foods by their nutrients. Learning why foods are grouped this way will help Terri make wise food choices now and all through her life.

Look at the picture of the foods in the pyramid. It shows how the foods you eat are divided into five

FIND OUT

What can I do to have more healthful eating habits?

▸ Talk with family members about the foods all of you eat and why you eat them.

▸ Refer to Unit A, pages A62–72, which discuss your teeth and their care.

▸ Read "An Interview with a Clinical Dietitian" on page B74.

▸ Explore the activities and gather information from pages B8–12.

basic food groups. Each group makes up part of this food pyramid. Here are the five food groups:

- Milk, Yogurt, and Cheese Group
- Meat, Poultry, Fish, Dry Beans, Eggs, and Nuts Group
- Vegetable Group
- Fruit Group
- Bread, Cereal, Rice, and Pasta Group

SCIENCE *connection*

FOOD ADVERTISEMENTS

On Your Own • The next time you watch television or read a magazine, list the different foods you see advertised. Decide in which food groups these foods belong. Make a data table to show your findings.

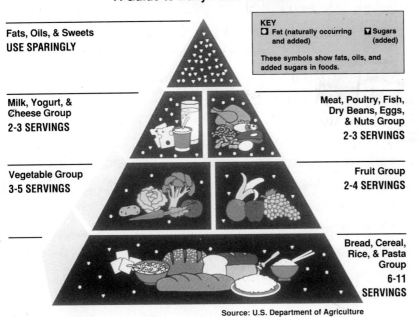

Food Guide Pyramid
A Guide to Daily Food Choices

Fats, Oils, & Sweets
USE SPARINGLY

KEY
☐ Fat (naturally occurring and added)
▼ Sugars (added)

These symbols show fats, oils, and added sugars in foods.

Milk, Yogurt, & Cheese Group
2-3 SERVINGS

Meat, Poultry, Fish, Dry Beans, Eggs, & Nuts Group
2-3 SERVINGS

Vegetable Group
3-5 SERVINGS

Fruit Group
2-4 SERVINGS

Bread, Cereal, Rice, & Pasta Group
6-11 SERVINGS

Source: U.S. Department of Agriculture

Foods in the Fruit Group and the Vegetable Group contain carbohydrates, vitamins, minerals, and fiber. The Meat, Poultry, Fish, Dry Beans, Eggs, and Nuts Group gives you mostly proteins and fats, along with vitamins, minerals, and fiber. The Milk, Yogurt, and Cheese Group provides nutrients for building strong bones and teeth. Foods in this group are a major source of proteins, water, vitamins, and minerals—mainly calcium. The Bread, Cereal, Rice, and Pasta Group gives your body carbohydrates as well as vitamins, minerals, and fiber.

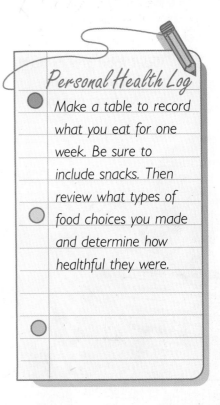

Personal Health Log

Make a table to record what you eat for one week. Be sure to include snacks. Then review what types of food choices you made and determine how healthful they were.

Project checkup

What information about food groups do you want to include in your food display?

Foods from the five basic food groups need to be your first choices in planning your diet. After that, you might select a few other foods. These other foods are sometimes grouped together as the Fats, Oils, and Sweets Group. Fats, oils, and sweets have fewer nutrients than foods in the five basic food groups. Foods in the Fats, Oils, and Sweets Group are high in fats and carbohydrates but low in proteins, vitamins, and minerals. These foods include cakes, cookies, salad dressings, and sweetened soft drinks. Eating too many of these foods may keep you from eating enough nutrients from foods in the five basic groups. Eating too much fat can cause you to gain extra weight. Eating a lot of sweets can raise your chances of tooth decay.

How Can You Balance Your Diet?

The food pyramid can help you plan meals having a variety of healthful foods. You can be sure that you are getting all the nutrients you need by eating foods from all the groups. When you eat the right amounts of foods from the five basic food groups each day, you have a **balanced diet.**

Yesterday Luis ate foods from each of the five basic food groups. For breakfast Luis had a bowl of cereal, two slices of toast, half a grapefruit, and a glass of orange juice. At lunchtime Luis ate a turkey sandwich, carrots, a pear, and had a glass of milk. For dinner Luis had broiled fish, green beans, a baked potato, and a glass of milk. He enjoyed eating a muffin for dessert.

Luis tried to have a balance of nutrients needed for good health. How will Luis know that he had a balanced diet?

■ The five basic food groups can help you plan meals with variety and a balance of nutrients.

The table shows how many servings from each food group you need to eat each day to have a balanced diet. A **serving** is the amount of a food that one person would be likely to eat during a meal.

A GUIDE FOR DAILY FOOD CHOICES

Food Group	Number of servings	Examples of servings
Bread, Cereal, Rice, and Pasta	6– 11 servings	1 slice bread 1 ounce dry cereal 1/2 cup cooked cereal, rice or pasta
Vegetable	3– 5 servings	1 cup raw, leafy vegetables 1/2 cup cooked or chopped raw vegetables 3/4 cup vegetable juice
Fruit	2– 4 servings	1 medium-sized apple, banana, or orange 1/2 cup chopped, cooked, or canned fruit 3/4 cup fruit juice
Milk, Yogurt, and Cheese	2– 3 servings	1 cup milk or yogurt 1 1/2 ounce natural cheese 2 ounces processed cheese
Meat, Poultry, Fish, Dry Beans, Eggs, and Nuts	2– 3 servings	2–3 ounces cooked lean meat, poultry, or fish 1/2 cup cooked dry beans, 1 egg, or 2 tablespoons peanut butter count as 1 ounce lean meat

ART connection

CLASSIFYING FOODS

With a Team • Construct a three-dimensional model of the Food Guide Pyramid out of cardboard. Cut out pictures of foods from magazines for each of the five basic food groups and place them on your pyramid. Refer to page B9, which shows the Food Guide Pyramid.

How Have Snacks Changed?

Think back to a time in history when most snacks did not come in packages. What did people eat then as snacks? People ate some of the very same snacks that you eat. They liked fresh or dried fruits, such as berries, apples, and apricots. These are foods with a variety of nutrients. Today, you have a much larger variety of fruits from which to choose. Pineapples, bananas, and fresh oranges would have been a real treat for children long ago. Back then, these fruits were grown in countries far from the United States.

Another difference between today and long ago is that in the past, children could eat fruits only when they were ripe enough to be picked or after they had been dried. Because of modern ways of freezing and canning foods, you can now eat most fruits all year. Unlike children many years ago, you have snack food choices other than fruits. You have to decide every day whether or not you should eat certain packaged snack foods. Some snack foods help you stay healthy. Others do not. Are the snack foods you eat healthful?

CHECK IT OUT!

How can you improve upon the choices you make concerning the foods you eat? Read the article on pages B84–87 in the Find Out Resource Center.

REFLECT

Information Check
1. What are the five basic food groups?
2. How might eating certain snacks help you stay healthy?

Solving Problems
3. Luis's turkey sandwich included foods from several food groups. What can you prepare for lunch that includes foods from more than one group?

Setting Goals
4. What can you do to control the amounts of fats in your daily diet?

B12

3 Deciding What to Eat

Knowing about nutrients, food groups, and a balanced diet should help you understand why you need to eat healthful foods. It should also help you know the kinds of food you need to eat to stay healthy. But even when you know these things, making decisions about food is not always easy.

How Can You Make Wise Food Choices?

Have you ever thought about *how* people decide what food to buy or eat? Sometimes people make choices so fast that they do not think about what they are doing. Here are some steps you can follow to make wise food choices:

1. Find out all you can about the choices you could make.
2. Think of the results of each possible choice.
3. Make what seems to be the best choice.
4. Think about what happens as a result of your choice.

FIND OUT

How can I learn to make healthful food choices?

▶Interview a cafeteria worker about food choices. Then make a checklist that might help you in making healthful food choices.
▶Explore the activities and gather information from pages B13–19.

CHECK IT OUT!

Make a balanced snack. On pieces of celery, spread peanut butter and add raisins. On other celery pieces, spread ricotta cheese made with skim milk and add a topping of unsweetened pineapple. Serve with whole-wheat crackers.

Maria sees that she needs to make a choice about what to drink with her lunch. She first finds out about different drinks she could choose. She does this by gathering facts about each kind of drink. She looks at the drink list and asks herself some questions: Have I ever bought this drink before? What do I know about this drink? By answering questions such as these, Maria gets the facts she needs to make a wise choice.

BEVERAGES

MILK	30
LOW-FAT MILK	25
ORANGE JUICE	35

■ *Maria needs to make a healthful food choice.*

Sometimes people can get more facts from a parent or friend. The more facts Maria has, the better prepared she is to make a choice. With facts, Maria can begin to think about the results of each possible choice. She asks herself, How will each drink keep me healthy?

Maria chooses the drink she thinks is best for her health. She chooses low-fat milk. When Maria tastes the low-fat milk, she says that she likes this kind of milk. Maria thinks about her choice. She seems happy with it and the way she made her choice.

Health Skill • Decision Making

Justin is preparing for a weekend outing with his Scout troop. Mr. Boles, the scoutmaster, has made plans for the outing. The troop will spend two nights at a ranch west of the city. Mr. Boles told Justin and the troop that he needs their help with the meals. They are pleased about this. It shows that Mr. Boles trusts them.

The troop will eat two dinners, two lunches, and two breakfasts on the outing. Mr. Boles asked the troop to plan meals that contain a variety of foods. The meals must also be balanced.

 What could Justin and his Scout troop plan for each meal?

Where Can You Find Facts About Food?

How can you find out which nutrients are in a package of food? Jason finds out what kinds of nutrients are in his foods by looking at the labels. You can, too.

Nutrition is the way your body uses food. Food labels give nutrition facts. Nutrition facts on a food label tell you each of the nutrients in the food. The label lists the vitamins and minerals found in the food. You can learn how much of each vitamin or mineral there is in your food by checking the label.

A food label will also give you information about ingredients. **Ingredients** are materials used to make the food. The ingredients are listed in a certain order. The list begins with the ingredient there is the most of.

■ *Labels provide nutritional information.*

It ends with the ingredient there is the least of. The list must include everything that is in the food.

Food labels may also describe how the food can help you plan a healthful diet. The label may say "good source of fiber," "low fat," or "fat free."

Reading food labels can help you learn to choose foods you need to stay healthy.

IT'S ALL IN THE LABEL

With a Partner • Collect labels for three to five food items that could make up a meal. Calculate to find the total number of grams of fat, protein, and dietary fiber you would consume if you ate the entire meal.

Nutrition Facts

Serving Size 2 cookies (27 g)
Servings Per Container 6

Amount Per Serving

Calories 110 Calories from Fat 25

	% Daily Value *
Total Fat 2.5g	**4%**
Saturated Fat 0g	**1%**
Polyunsaturated Fat 0.5g	
Monounsaturated Fat 0.5g	
Cholesterol 0mg	**0%**
Sodium 135mg	**6%**
Total Carbohydrate 20g	**7%**
Dietary Fiber 1g	**3%**
Sugars 10g	
Protein 2g	

Vitamin A 0%	•	Vitamin C 0%
Calcium 2%	•	Iron 4%

* Percent Daily Values are based on a 2,000 calorie diet. Your daily values may be higher or lower depending on your calorie needs:

		Calories:	2,000	2,500
Total Fat	Less than		65g	80g
Sat Fat	Less than		20g	25g
Cholesterol	Less than		300mg	300mg
Sodium	Less than		2400mg	2400mg
Total Carbohydrate			300g	375g
Dietary Fiber			25g	30g

INGREDIENTS: ENRICHED WHEAT FLOUR (CONTAINS NIACIN, REDUCED IRON, THIAMINE MONONITRATE [VITAMIN B$_1$], RIBOFLAVIN [VITAMIN B$_2$]), RAISINS, SUGAR, ROLLED OATS, VEGETABLE SHORTENING (PARTIALLY HYDROGENATED CANOLA OIL), OAT FLOUR, LEAVENING (BAKING SODA, SODIUM ALUMINUM PHOSPHATE, CALCIUM PHOSPHATE), EMULSIFIERS (SOY LECITHIN, SODIUM STEAROYL LACTYLATE, DIACETYL TARTARIC ACID ESTERS OF MONOGLYCERIDES), SALT, WHEY, NATURAL AND ARTIFICIAL FLAVOR, CINNAMON, EGG WHITES.

Personal Health Log

Are You Making Healthful Food Choices?

How do you know if you are making wise food choices? You might not be if any of the following statements describe you. If they do, talk about improving your food choices with a parent, guardian, school nurse, or teacher.

- You eat few fresh fruits and vegetables.

- You do not eat breakfast every morning.
- You most often eat sweet cereal as your breakfast food.
- You eat only a few kinds of food.
- Sweetened soft drinks are your favorite snacks.

Some food package labels have more information. They tell you where the food was packaged. Many of the foods that Jason's parents buy come from places far away from their home. Fresh foods, such as potatoes, are packed in boxes or bags that show where the foods were grown. Most potatoes come from either Idaho or Maine. Most oranges come from Florida, Texas, or California. Texas onions, cabbages, watermelons, and beef are sold all over the country. So are Washington apples, Louisiana rice, Georgia peanuts, and Iowa pork.

FOODS GROWN IN THE UNITED STATES

Salmon — ALASKA

Apples — WASHINGTON

Potatoes — IDAHO

Wheat

Potatoes — MAINE

Mushrooms — PENNSYLVANIA

IOWA Pork

Corn — INDIANA

Beef

California

Grapes

ARKANSAS

LOUISIANA RICE

TEXAS

Peanuts — GEORGIA

Onions

FLORIDA — Oranges

HAWAII

Pineapple

B17

How Can You Avoid Unsafe Foods?

Maria drinks low-fat milk at home and at school. One day she poured a glass of cold milk at home. She soon noticed that the milk did not smell as it should. Maria decided not to drink the milk. She asked her father why the milk had a bad smell. Her father smelled the milk and told Maria that it was spoiled. Spoiled food is food that is not safe to eat or drink because it can make you ill. Milk will spoil if it is not kept in a refrigerator at home and at the store.

Spoiled milk has a bad smell and does not taste good. Other spoiled foods look different than they do when they are fresh. Spoiled bread, for example, might be covered with black or green mold. Mold is a living organism that grows on some spoiled foods.

However, you cannot always tell when a food is spoiled. Some foods, such as chicken, may not smell, taste, or look different when they are spoiled. It is also hard to decide about foods that are inside cans. A bad dent or a bulge in a can may mean the food inside is spoiled, but you cannot be sure. If you think a food might be spoiled, tell an adult or throw the food away. Do not take chances with your health by eating foods you think might be spoiled.

■ Some food naturally spoils after a few days. The date printed on this carton tells you the milk should be sold on or before that date.

■ Why might these foods be unsafe to eat?

B18

Food that is not handled properly can become spoiled. Here are some tips for making sure the food you will eat does not spoil:

- Always wash your hands before touching food you are preparing and before you eat.
- Always use clean eating and drinking utensils.
- Keep foods such as milk and meat in the refrigerator.
- Refrigerate leftovers right away.
- Do not eat any food that looks spoiled or smells different from the way it normally does.
- Always read the label before you buy a product.

■ Washing your hands before handling food helps keep germs from spreading.

REFLECT

Information Check

1. What information do food package labels provide?
2. What four steps can you use in making wise food choices?
3. How might a can look if the food inside is spoiled?

Solving Problems

4. Suppose you buy meat, eggs, canned soup, flour, and oatmeal at the grocery store. Which of these foods need special storage when you get home? Why?

Setting Goals

5. What goals can you set for using food labeling to plan healthful meals?

Project checkup

What information on safe food handling do you want to include in your food display?

SHARE

You have gathered a lot of information about how food provides you with energy and how healthful eating habits and good food choices can help you grow. Think of ways you can share something you have learned with others. Here are some ideas:

▶ Share with your classmates what you learned about making healthful food choices while working on your project.

▶ Set up your food display in the school cafeteria so that other students can benefit from what you learned.

▶ Work with your classmates to find more ways to share your knowledge about healthful food choices.

HEALTHY FOOD CHOICES

FATS
OILS
SWEETS
USE SPARINGLY

MILK,
YOGURT,
CHEESE
GROUP
2-3 SERVINGS

MEAT, FISH,
POULTRY,
DRY BEANS,
EGGS, NUT
2-3 SERVINGS

VEGETABLE
GROUP
3-5 SERVINGS

FRUIT
GROUP
2-4 SERVINGS

BREAD, CEREAL, RICE AND PASTA
GROUP
6-11 SERVINGS

ACT

Health is more than gathering information—it is making wise choices and practicing good health habits. How might you use what you have learned about healthful food choices? Here are some things you can do for . . .

Yourself

▶ Write to the U.S. Food and Drug Administration (FDA), see page B99. Ask for information about food additives.

▶ Check the labels on snacks you plan to eat to be sure they are healthful snacks.

Your Family

▶ Discuss with your family what you have learned, and together plan how you can improve your diet.

Your School and Community

▶ Make posters about healthful eating habits and ways to make healthful food choices and display them at school or a local grocery store.

What will you do?

Joseph Gomez
15 Arbol Street
San Diego, CA 52723

U.S. Food and Drug Administration (FDA)
Office of Consumer Affairs, Public Inquiries
5600 Fishers Lane (HFE-88)
Rockville, MD 20857

EXERCISE, REST, AND SLEEP

Fitness is for everyone. All people need healthy bodies that work at their best. People need healthy hearts and lungs. They need strong muscles and bones. People meet their fitness needs with proper exercise, posture, rest, and sleep. How you choose to meet your fitness needs can affect your health while you are young. The way you meet your fitness needs now can also affect your wellness for a lifetime.

ASK QUESTIONS

How can physical fitness affect my health?
Why do I need rest and sleep?
How can exercise help me stay physically fit?
What questions do *you* have?

Project

Write a Script for a Fitness Video

With a Team • Write a script for a fitness video. Be sure your script includes directions for at least 20 minutes of vigorous exercise that you can recommend doing three times a week. You can write your script for the video as you learn more about fitness in this section. Working on your script will help answer your questions.

B23

1 Building an Active You

Think about the things you like to do at play. Do you like to run? Perhaps you like to swim, skate, or play ball with friends. All those things can be fun. Being active at play can also help you stay healthy.

What Is Exercise?

Most of Danny's days are active. She walks to school. She plays kickball at recess. During physical education class this month, her class is doing fitness training. After school she takes swimming lessons. All those activities make Danny's body work hard. Any activity that makes the body work hard is called **exercise.**

FIND OUT

How can physical fitness affect my health?

▶ Ask a fitness instructor questions about physical fitness and health.

▶ Talk to an adult family member about how exercise and physical fitness affect your health.

▶ Refer to pages A38–42 and pages A46–47, in Unit A, which discuss how your skeletal, muscular, and respiratory systems work.

▶ Explore the activities and gather information from pages B24–35.

■ Exercising with your friends is fun. Exercises such as running and climbing help you stay healthy.

When your body works hard during play, you are exercising. Exercise can make your heart and other muscles strong. It makes you breathe faster and more deeply. It makes oxygen and nutrients in your blood move faster through your circulatory system to all the cells in your body.

■ *Exercising with your friends is fun. Exercises such as running and climbing help you stay healthy.*

CHECK IT OUT!

There are many resources that can help you find answers to your questions. Be sure to consult the Find Out Resource Center on pages B70–99.

Daily play and exercise help you reach physical fitness. **Physical fitness** means having your body work the best it can. When your body works at its best, you are physically fit. Being physically fit helps you look and feel healthy. Looking and feeling healthy help you build a positive self-concept.

■ *All people benefit from exercise.*

How Can Physical Fitness Help You?

Having physical fitness means you have enough energy to do your daily work. You can play in lively games without tiring too quickly. Reaching physical fitness is something you have to do yourself. You are responsible for keeping your body healthy by having it work at its best.

■ *Exercise increases the heartbeat rate, which can be measured as your pulse. A pulse is the flow of blood through certain blood vessels, such as those in the wrist.*

Your body works best when it has the energy and oxygen it needs. You get energy from nutrients in the food you eat. You get oxygen from air you breathe. Your circulatory system carries nutrients and oxygen to your cells, tissues, and organs.

Your heart pumps blood throughout your body. Active play and exercise make your heart strong. Then it can work its best. Each time your heart beats, it pushes blood through your circulatory system. A fit heart beats more slowly because it can pump more blood each time it beats. This push of blood through your blood vessels with each heartbeat creates your **pulse.**

Before Mrs. Jenkins had begun playing tennis three times a week, she counted her pulse while she was sitting quietly. She found that her heart beat about 70 times a minute. After playing tennis for three months, three or four times every week, Mrs. Jenkins has a heart rate of only 60 times a minute when she is sitting still. The slower pulse rate shows that her heart has become stronger. Regular exercise has made Mrs. Jenkins's heart muscle stronger, and she is more physically fit.

LANGUAGE ARTS connection

DAILY ACTIVITIES

On Your Own • List ten ways you can add to the amount of daily exercise you get. Riding a bicycle or walking instead of riding in a car or bus may be one way. Helping with some kinds of active household chores may be another.

SCIENCE connection

TAKING YOUR PULSE

On Your Own • Gently press your first and second fingers against the inside of your wrist, below your thumb. You should be able to feel beats caused by your heart. Count the heartbeats you feel in one minute. This number is your pulse rate. Refer to Unit A, pages A50–51, which discuss your circulatory system. With your finger, trace the path that blood takes through the circulatory system to the wrist.

How Is Food Related to Exercise?

There is a connection between food and exercise. One way you can see this is in your weight.

The amount and kind of food you eat and the amount and kind of exercise you get need to be in balance. If they are in balance, your weight will stay about the same. If you eat more food than your body can use, you will gain weight. If you need to change your weight, you can change the amount of food you eat. You can also change the amount of exercise you get. Before making any weight changes, however, you need to talk with a parent, a guardian, your school nurse, or a physician.

■ *To maintain a healthful weight, you need a balance of diet and exercise.*

Personal Health Log

Do You Have Healthful Fitness Habits?

How do you know whether you are developing healthful exercise and fitness habits? Ask yourself whether each of the following statements applies to you. Record your answers. If you say no to any of the statements, you might need to improve your habits. You should talk about this with a parent, guardian, school nurse, or teacher.

■ You exercise vigorously for 20 to 30 minutes at least three times each week.

■ You use exercise to relieve tension and worry.

■ When lifting something heavy, you use your legs and arms, not your back.

■ You practice good posture when you stand, sit, and walk.

■ You do different kinds of exercises to improve your endurance, strength, and flexibility.

How Can Muscle Strength Help You?

Yoshi, Neal, and Erica exercise each day. They know that exercise helps keep their bodies physically fit. Regular exercise helps Yoshi, Neal, and Erica be physically fit in three important ways. First, exercise makes their muscles, including their hearts, stronger. It also makes them able to be active longer without getting tired. Finally, exercise makes it easier for them to move and twist their bodies.

Yoshi rides her bicycle about 20 minutes every day. When she rides her bicycle, she has fun. She is also exercising. Exercising each day helps Yoshi build muscle strength. When you have **muscle strength,** your body is able to apply force with its muscles.

By riding her bicycle, Yoshi builds strength in her leg muscles. The more Yoshi exercises her leg muscles, the stronger her muscles become. Strong leg muscles make it easier for Yoshi to ride her bicycle up hills and for long distances. Also, Yoshi's heart becomes stronger as she rides her bicycle.

LANGUAGE ARTS *connection*

EXERCISE EQUIPMENT

With a Team • Collect advertisements for exercise equipment, and use them to make a display. Read each advertisement to see what it claims the equipment will do for you. Do you think a person could get the same health benefits by exercising without the equipment?

■ *Some forms of exercise increase muscle strength. Bicycling strengthens Yoshi's leg muscles and her heart.*

B29

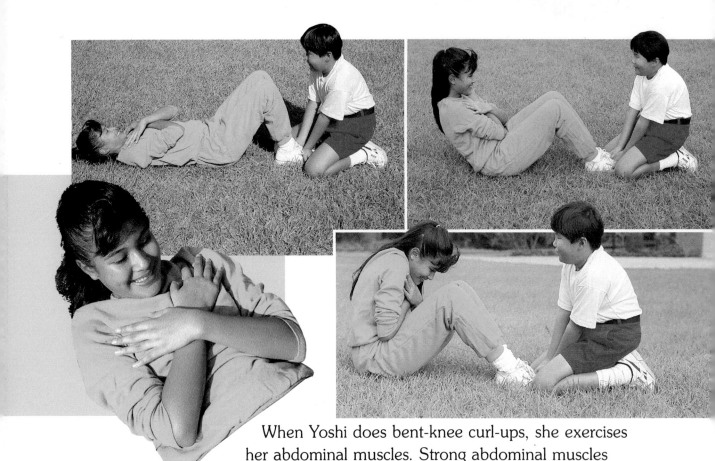

■ *Bent-knee curl-ups strengthen Yoshi's abdominal muscles.*

Project ✓
checkup

What types of exercises will you include in the script for your fitness video?

When Yoshi does bent-knee curl-ups, she exercises her abdominal muscles. Strong abdominal muscles make it easier for Yoshi to sit up and lie back down again.

You need to be active in different ways to exercise different muscles. Then all your muscles become stronger.

You need strong muscles to have good posture. **Posture** is the way you hold your body. Strong muscles help hold your spine straight while you sit, walk, and stand. Strong muscles help your back and legs hold up your body weight. Good posture makes you look good. Standing, sitting, and walking with good posture also shows others that you feel good about yourself.

Weak muscles can cause poor posture. Weak muscles can get stiff easily. They can make parts of your body ache. They can also cause you to slump your shoulders or your back. Then your muscles may tire. Walking with poor posture also can make muscles sore.

Using good posture should be a daily habit. It is easier when you have strong muscles.

■ *Good posture helps you look and feel better. Poor posture shows you do not care about yourself.*

What Is Endurance?

Ten weeks ago, Neal could jump rope for only one minute. He became tired very quickly. He decided he would jump rope each day. He slowly raised the time he could jump rope to 5 minutes each day. He kept raising the time a little more each week. After eight weeks, Neal was jumping rope every day for 20 minutes without stopping.

Over the past ten weeks, Neal has improved his physical endurance. **Endurance** is the ability to be active a long time without getting too tired to keep going. Neal keeps up his endurance by jumping rope often and by being active in other ways.

Jumping rope helped build Neal's endurance by making his heart and his arm and leg muscles strong. It also helped his lungs move more air into and out of his body. The better Neal's lungs work, the better his body is able to work while exercising.

FITNESS FOR WELLNESS POSTER

On Your Own • Make a fitness poster, and put it up in your home. Your poster might illustrate some way in which regular exercise contributes to wellness. Or it might show several exercises that increase a person's endurance, strength, and flexibility.

Neal needs extra energy to jump rope for a long time. His muscles get energy from the nutrients stored in his body. As Neal jumps rope, he breathes faster and deeper. He breathes in extra oxygen. The oxygen is pumped to his muscles by a faster, stronger heartbeat (pulse). The quicker pulse sends stored nutrients to working muscles faster.

When Neal stops jumping rope, he still breathes hard, but only for a short time. Because he is doing less work, he needs less oxygen. Neal recovers quickly and breathes easily after exercising hard. He has good endurance.

Jumping rope is one of the activities that make your lungs and heart work hard. Many of these activities are fun. What other activities can make your lungs and heart work hard? Activities that cause you to breathe deeply and your heart to beat quickly for at least 20 minutes are called **aerobic exercises.** Aerobic exercises are done at a medium pace so that they can be done for a long time without stopping. Aerobic exercises help you build endurance. They make your heart, other muscles, and lungs physically fit. By doing 20 to 30 minutes of aerobic exercise at least three times a week, you can help make your body work at its best. You can develop endurance, and you can become physically fit.

■ Distance running is another aerobic exercise that builds endurance.

How Can Being Flexible Help You?

When Erica started learning to dance, she found it hard to bend, twist, and stretch. Her body felt stiff. Now she can move smoothly without feeling sore. Stretching before and after dancing helped Erica become more flexible. Being **flexible** means being able to move your joints easily and without tightness or pain.

Erica keeps up her flexibility by stretching before each time she dances. She sits on the floor with her legs straight. Then she bends forward. In that way, she stretches her leg muscles. Erica has learned that being flexible makes it less likely that her muscles will become sore or injured.

Stretching is part of Erica's warm-up before she dances. During a **warm-up,** you slowly start exercising.

SCIENCE
connection

SURVEY OF EXERCISE HABITS

With a Partner • Make an exercise chart. Ask your classmates to list the kinds of exercise they do. Then mark on the chart whether the exercise is good for endurance, strength, or flexibility.

A five-minute warm-up gets your muscles ready to work. Stretching is part of a good warm-up. Stretching and other easy exercises increase the pulse little by little so that more blood flows to the muscles.

Erica also stretches after dancing. Stretching for five minutes after exercise acts as a cool-down activity.

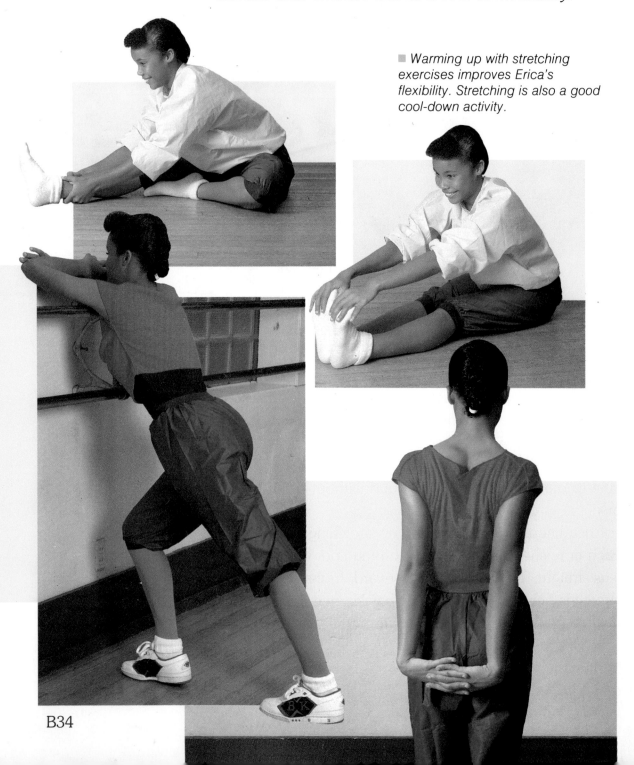

■ Warming up with stretching exercises improves Erica's flexibility. Stretching is also a good cool-down activity.

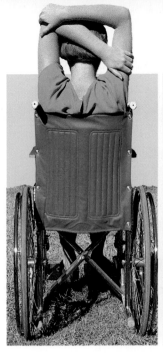

■ *Stretching helps Melissa warm up her arms for the task of moving her wheelchair.*

During a **cool-down,** you slowly stop exercising. Stretching, slowly pedaling a bicycle, or walking are good for a cool-down. A cool-down lets your muscles slowly relax as your pulse returns to normal.

You need to warm up before aerobic exercise and cool down afterwards. If you do, your play and exercise will be safer and more healthful.

REFLECT

Information Check
1. Why is playing kickball exercise?
2. Why is exercise important in your life?

Solving Problems
3. Suppose you have not ridden your bicycle for six weeks. You see a notice for a 10-mile (16-kilometer) bicycle ride to be held in your community tomorrow. Should you go? Explain your answer.

Setting Goals
4. A good health goal is to have physical fitness all your life. What are some things you can do now to help yourself reach that goal?

Personal Health Log

On a chart, record when, how, and how long you exercise during one week. At the end of the week, evaluate how well you did.

2 Rest and Sleep

No matter how fit you are, you still get tired. Just as your body needs regular exercise, it needs regular rest and sleep. While you rest and sleep, your body stores the energy it will use for work and play. After resting and sleeping, you have the energy you need to be active again. To help keep yourself physically fit, you need a daily balance of exercise, rest, and sleep.

Why Do You Need Rest and Quiet?

Kiyo is active most of the day. By late afternoon, she starts to feel tired. Feeling tired helps Kiyo's body protect itself from working too hard. It lets Kiyo know that her body needs rest.

When you rest, your body slows down and uses less energy. Resting gives your heart, other muscles, and lungs a chance to **relax,** or become calm. After you have been active for a long time, your muscles often get tight. They can feel sore. Resting helps your muscles relax. They loosen up and help your body get the rest it needs. As you rest, your pulse slows down, and you breathe slowly and easily.

Sitting quietly by yourself is one way of resting to relax. Other ways are reading for pleasure, playing board games with friends or parents, or even daydreaming after school.

FIND OUT

Why do I need rest and sleep?

▶ Invite a physician to visit your class and talk about the importance of rest and sleep.

▶ Ask family members to recall how they felt when they did not get enough sleep or rest.

▶ Explore the activities and gather information from pages B36–38.

Project checkup

How are rest and sleep a part of the script for your project?

Every day, you also need the rest that comes only from sleep. When you sleep, your whole body rests, including your brain.

Why Do You Need Sleep?

Scientists do not know exactly why people need to sleep. But everyone must sleep for part of each day. If people go without sleep for a few days, they will become ill.

When you sleep, your whole body rests. But it does not stop working. It still uses energy, but less than when you are awake. When you sleep, your body is working to store energy for being active the next day.

You are responsible for staying fit by getting enough sleep. When you get enough sleep, you are helping to keep yourself healthy. How much sleep a person needs depends partly on age. When you were a baby, you needed more sleep than you do now. Most people your age need between 10 and 11 hours of sleep each night. Some adults need only between 5 and 6 hours of sleep.

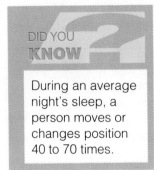

DID YOU **KNOW**

During an average night's sleep, a person moves or changes position 40 to 70 times.

MATH *connection*

FIGURING YOUR SHUT-EYE TIME

On Your Own •
Write down the number of hours of sleep you get each night for one week. Add up the figures, and then divide by seven. How many hours of sleep do you get, on the average, each night? How do you know whether you are getting enough sleep?

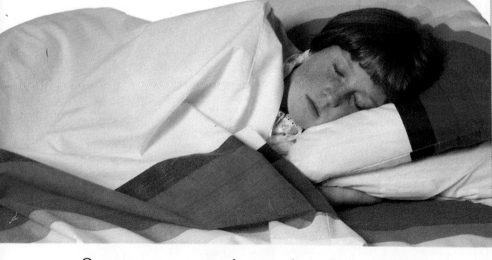

One reason you need more sleep than older people is that you are probably more active than they are. Another reason is that your body is still growing. You need a lot of energy to be active and to grow.

■ *Sleep helps your whole body rest and store energy for the next day.*

CHECK IT OUT!

Does fast walking give you better exercise than jogging or running? Use library books and magazines to help you find information on fast walking.

Information Check

1. About how many hours of sleep do people your age need each night?
2. Why do young people need more sleep than most adults?

Solving Problems

3. Ashley often feels sleepy in class. What can she do to deal with this problem?

Setting Goals

4. How do you plan to get the proper amount of rest that your body needs?

Personal Health Log

Are You Making Healthful Choices About Rest, Sleep, Posture, and Exercise?

Make a chart like the one shown here. On your chart, check off each day that you

1. take time to rest or relax during the day.
2. get at least 10 hours of sleep at night.
3. try to sit and stand straight and tall.
4. play actively for 20 to 30 minutes without stopping.

Think of yourself doing each activity. Describe on the chart how each activity affects your muscles and lungs. Think about how these activities help a person stay physically fit.

Healthful Choices Chart							
	Sunday	Monday	Tuesday	Wednesday	Thursday	Friday	Saturday
Rested + relaxed							
10 - 11 hours sleep							
Sit and stand tall							
Play actively 20-30 minutes							

3 Choices You Make to Be Fit

Maybe you want to play active games more often to help your body work at its best. You want to exercise more to feel good about yourself. But your body may not be used to the exercise. You need to increase the amount you exercise little by little. You need to get a good start so that you will enjoy your new health habit.

How Do You Start Exercising?

All people need active exercise. But people start exercising in different ways. Check with your parents, physical education teacher, or school nurse to find out what exercise to do and how much to do. Then increase slowly. Do just a little more exercise each day. After three or four weeks, you should be able to exercise for a longer time. You should be able to exercise for 20 to 30 minutes without resting.

If you choose the right kind of exercise, you will become stronger. You will have more endurance.

■ *Start an exercise routine slowly. Begin by exercising for a short time each day. Then gradually increase the amount until you can exercise for 20 to 30 minutes without resting.*

FIND OUT

How can exercise help me stay physically fit?

▶ Invite a fitness instructor to visit your class.
▶ Interview five classmates and find out what they do to stay physically fit.
▶ Read "Questions for a Physical Education Teacher" on page B76.
▶ Refer to pages B1–12, which discuss making healthful food choices.
▶ Explore the activities and gather information from pages B39–43.

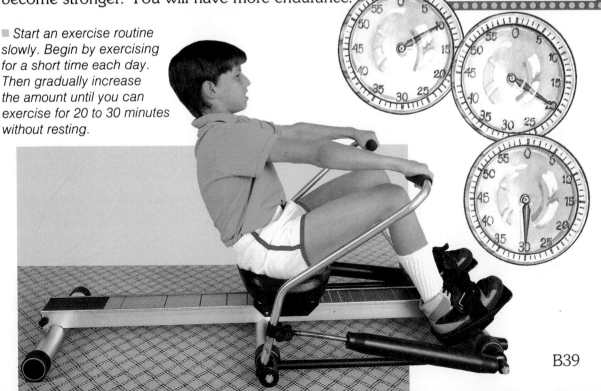

PHYSICAL EDUCATION *connection*

EXERCISE ROUTINE

With a Team • Make up an exercise routine. Each of you should choose one or two simple exercises to do, such as jumping jacks or sit-ups. Choose music to accompany your routine. Perform your exercise routine, and teach it to the rest of the class.

LANGUAGE ARTS *connection*

COMPARING YOUR FITNESS

On Your Own • Find out how physically fit you are. Ask a physical education teacher about the FYT (Fit Youth Today) Program. Write to the American Health and Fitness Foundation, 6225 U.S. Highway 290 E., Suite 114, Austin, TX 78723.

Your body will become more flexible. It is possible to choose exercises that will help you build strength, endurance, and flexibility all at the same time. What, do you think, are some of those exercises?

Staying physically fit is an important responsibility for young people and adults. Choose activities you enjoy. Feeling good about what you do will make it easy for you to keep exercising. Some people choose activities that they will enjoy all their lives. Lynn's father learned to swim when he was in the fourth grade. He still makes time to swim several days a week. He goes swimming either before or after work. Lynn's father chose a way to stay fit that has helped him stay healthy as he grows older.

There are exercises you can enjoy doing alone. Some exercises can be done with one other person or with a group of family members or friends. There are exercises that do not require special clothes. There are different exercises for people with different talents. Some people enjoy gymnastics. Others are good at tennis. People with physical handicaps also enjoy exercises that suit them. Some people who are blind can snow-ski. Some people in wheelchairs play basketball.

By setting a goal of daily exercise, you choose a way to stay healthy. Meeting your fitness goal will help you feel good about yourself. Exercise helps many people relax and feel good.

■ *Some games can be fun for the entire family, as well as help you relax.*

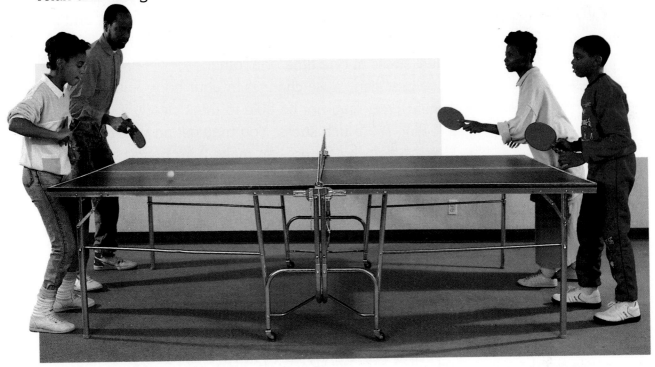

Health Skill • Decision Making

Alex is active with his classmates in physical education class. He runs, bends, and stretches. During recess he sometimes plays tag. Alex also likes to watch sports on television. He watches games on television for many hours each week. When friends ask him to play an active game, Alex always says he is too busy. Sometimes he tells his friends that he is too tired. He also says, "I don't need to play any games. I get plenty of exercise in physical education class."

? Is Alex making a wise decision? Why or why not?

How Can Exercise Help Fight Stress?

Stress is a tense feeling that you get, as if you were about to run or fight. You can feel stress from things that bother you. You can feel stress when you get into an argument. You can feel stress before, during, and after an exciting time, such as a class play. All people feel stress at one time or another.

Stress can cause changes in your body and your mind. You may not be able to think clearly if you are feeling too much stress. You may get an upset stomach or a headache. Stress can make your heart beat faster than it should while you are sitting still. Your muscles may feel tight.

Exercise is a good way to ease the body changes that come from stress. It helps your body get rid of the tense feelings. Exercise can also help take your mind off what caused your stress. After exercise you feel better—more relaxed—and you can think more clearly.

What Kinds of Exercise Can Help You Build Fitness?

Lively sports are good exercise for your whole body. Riding your bicycle, running, fast walking, cross-country skiing, and swimming are all very good aerobic exercises if done for at least 20 minutes without stopping.

SOCIAL STUDIES *connection*

GETTING ALONG WITH OTHERS

On Your Own • Tell how your play activities help you learn ways of getting along with others. Think about the rules in some games and the need for following those rules.

Project checkup

How will the information you have learned here help you act out your script for the exercise video?

■ *Being upset with yourself, or with someone else, causes stress. Exercise can often get rid of stress and make you feel better.*

They make your muscles work hard. They make you breathe hard. They make your heart beat fast. They also help ease the effects of stress.

People who dance or do gymnastics build strength in addition to endurance. They become more flexible. They stretch, swing, and jump. Exercising in these ways helps keep their bodies fit.

You are responsible for helping to keep yourself healthy and fit. Choosing the best ways to keep yourself fit can help your body all your life. Being responsible for fitness habits can make you feel good about yourself.

■ Gymnastics is a good activity to keep you fit. It builds muscle strength and endurance. It also increases flexibility.

REFLECT

Information Check

1. What should you do before changing your exercise habits? Why?
2. How does exercise help ease the effects of stress?

Solving Problems

3. Diego lives in northern Alaska, where he is not able to go outside much during the winter. Describe how Diego can still get exercise year-round.

Setting Goals

4. How do you plan to become physically fit?

SHARE

You have gathered a lot of information about exercise, rest, and sleep. Think of ways you can share with others something you have learned. Here are some ideas:

▶ Report to your class what you learned about exercise while working on your project.

▶ Team up with your classmates to develop a "Rainy-Day Fitness Center" in your classroom. Invent an indoor marching drill that lasts 15 to 20 minutes. Use a drum or other instrument to keep a rhythm.

▶ Show your classmates where to find important information on rest, exercise, and physical fitness.

ACT

Health is more than gathering information—it is making wise choices and practicing good health habits. How might you use what you have learned about exercise, rest, and sleep? Here are some things you can do for . . .

Yourself

▶ Design a chart that you can use to show your progress in attaining your physical fitness goals.

▶ Discuss with an adult family member or your teacher how you can develop physical fitness.

Your Family

▶ Plan with your family how exercise can be included in your daily routines.

Your School and Community

▶ Find out what kind of after-school recreational programs your community has available. Discuss with other students in your school what you have learned.

What will you do?

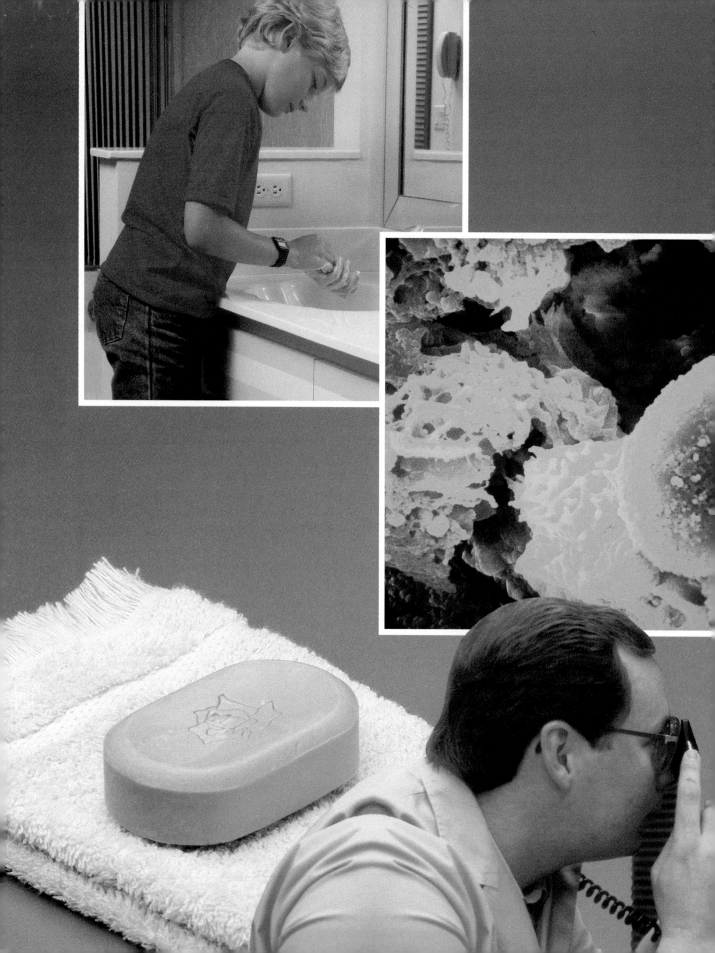

GUARDING AGAINST DISEASE

At one time or another, most of us have been ill. Your body has ways of fighting illness. There are ways you can help keep yourself from becoming ill. Practicing good health habits is one way. To protect your wellness, you need to help your body avoid illness.

ASK QUESTIONS

Why do people become ill?
What can I do to protect myself from disease?
What questions do you have?

Project

Disease Prevention Bulletin Board
With a Team • Develop a disease prevention bulletin board. Display information on the types of diseases covered in this section. In your display, include causes, symptoms, treatments, and preventive measures for each disease. Illustrate your display with drawings or photos from magazines. Add any other facts of interest you might think of. You and your team can cut out newspaper and magazine articles to put on the bulletin board in the appropriate areas.

1 Communicable Disease

Think of the people you see in school. Most of them go to school every day. They stay healthy most of the time. Their bodies work well more often than they do not. Your body probably works well most of the time, too. When your body is not working well, however, you feel ill.

FIND OUT

Why do people become ill?

▶ Make a list of questions you might ask your physician or another health care worker.

▶ Talk to family members about why people become ill.

▶ Look up diseases in a reference book, such as an encyclopedia.

▶ Explore the activities and gather information from pages B48–58.

■ *Your classmates stay healthy most of the time. However, sometimes illness keeps their bodies from working well.*

What Happens When Someone Gets Ill?

Sally is ill today. She has a cough and a sore throat. Her eyes are watery. Her body is warmer than usual. Sally has a disease. A **disease** is a breakdown in the way the body works. It means that some part of the body has stopped working as it should.

A disease may make a person feel discomfort and pain. A disease may cause other signs of illness.

B48

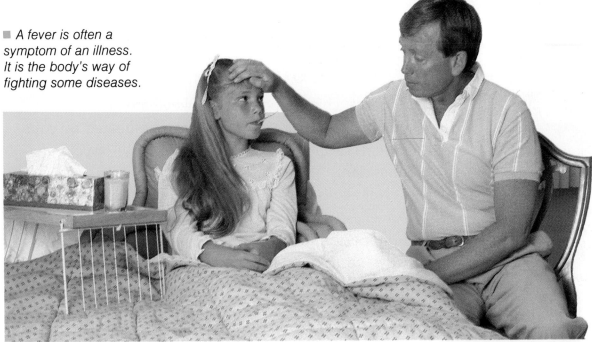

■ *A fever is often a symptom of an illness. It is the body's way of fighting some diseases.*

These signs of a disease are called its **symptoms.** Each disease has its own symptoms. The symptoms of a cold, for example, may be a cough, a sore throat, and a higher than normal body temperature.

When you have symptoms of a disease, you may need **treatment,** or care. Your parents might care for you at home. You might also need a physician's help. A physician can tell you what kind of disease you have. A physician can also tell your parents how to treat your disease. You might need to take medicine. Or your body might be strong enough to get well by itself in a short time.

What Kinds of Disease Are There?

Can you remember the last time you had a cold? Did someone you know have a cold before you got yours? Did someone else you know get a cold right after you?

A cold can spread from one person to another. Your cold most likely spread from someone to you. In turn, you might have spread the cold to another person. A cold is one example of a communicable disease.

SCIENCE *connection*

DISEASES AROUND YOU

With a Team • Check with your local or state department of health to find out if and when outbreaks of disease, called *epidemics*, have affected your community. Also find out what disease was involved, when the epidemic took place, and how many people were affected. Find out how future epidemics of the same disease can be avoided. Share your information with the class.

CHECK IT OUT!

How do healthful living habits and a balanced diet help prevent disease? You can find out by contacting your physician or local health department.

A **communicable disease** is an illness that can be spread from person to person. Water, food, and animals can spread some communicable diseases to people.

Colds, chicken pox, and pinkeye are all communicable diseases. They can be treated by your parents, with help from the school nurse or your physician.

Not all diseases are spread from person to person. An illness or a health problem that cannot be spread from person to person is a **noncommunicable disease.** Examples of noncommunicable diseases are heart disease and asthma.

Scientists who study disease do not always know why a person gets a certain noncommunicable disease. For some people, a family history of the disease is a reason. Scientists say that healthful living habits can help prevent some noncommunicable diseases. To **prevent** means to keep something from happening. Eating a balanced diet is one way to prevent certain diseases. Sleeping enough to feel rested and getting daily exercise will also help. Never smoking or chewing tobacco are two more ways of preventing many diseases.

■ *Some communicable diseases can be spread easily by coughing and sneezing.*

Many diseases, such as cancer and heart disease, last a long time. Some might last for months or years. Any disease that continues for a long time, usually more than a month, is said to be **chronic.** Other diseases last a short time, usually less than a month. They are called **acute.** An earache is an acute illness. A cold is another example of an acute illness.

Scientists are always looking for ways to prevent diseases. Learning and practicing good health habits can help you protect yourself against diseases. Learning the early warning signs of diseases can help, too. Checking with a physician as soon as those early signs appear can help keep a disease under control.

■ *Tell a parent when you are not feeling well. A parent can decide if you need to see a physician.*

SOCIAL STUDIES *connection*

DISEASE DISASTERS

With a Partner • There have been times in history when communicable and noncommunicable disease have made a tremendous impact on human populations. Use reference books to find out how diseases have affected history. Check on such topics as the Black Plague, the impact of measles on Native Americans, and the great influenza outbreak of 1918. Share with your classmates how the occurrences of these and other diseases might affect our lives today.

What Kinds of Microbes Cause Disease?

CHECK IT OUT!

You may need to consult other resources in order to find answers to your health questions. For ideas, check out the Find Out Resource Center on pages B70–99.

Germs cause communicable diseases. Germs are microbes that can make you ill. **Microbes** are living things so small that they can be seen only with a microscope. Thousands of microbes would fit in a single drop of water.

Some microbes are helpful to people. Some are neither helpful nor harmful. Others can cause disease. When you have disease microbes in your body, you have an infection. An **infection** is the growth of disease microbes somewhere in your body. When your body has an infection, you can sometimes become ill.

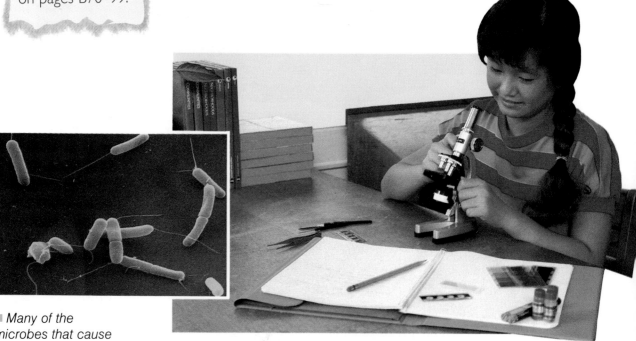

■ *Many of the microbes that cause disease, left, can be seen only with a microscope.*

Disease microbes can be grouped in many ways. Three main groups of disease microbes are viruses, bacteria, and fungi. Each group looks different from the others. Each kind of disease microbe in a group can cause a different communicable disease.

 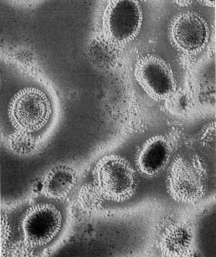 

■ *Viruses are very small. Shown here are viruses that cause chicken pox, left; flu, center; and measles, right.*

Viruses. The **viruses** make up one group of microbes. These are the smallest kind of disease microbes. A virus cannot live by itself. It needs to live inside the cells of some other creature. Some viruses live in people. Other viruses live in animals or in plants.

When a virus gets inside a living cell, it takes over the cell. It makes the cell stop doing its usual work. Instead, the cell starts making new viruses. When the cell is full of viruses, it breaks open. The viruses spill out and enter nearby healthy cells. Each of those cells then makes more viruses. In this way, one virus microbe soon turns into many virus microbes.

Some viruses cause diseases such as colds, chicken pox, and measles. Persons having some viruses that cause disease may not have any symptoms. HIV is one such virus. *HIV* stands for *human immunodeficiency virus.* This virus attacks certain blood cells and harms the body's ability to defend itself against other infections. HIV causes the disease AIDS. *AIDS* stands for *acquired immunodeficiency syndrome.* People with AIDS cannot fight off infections as well as healthy people can. These infections can be strong enough to cause a person's death.

MYTH
AND
FACT

Myth: A person can get AIDS by hugging or shaking hands.

Fact: The AIDS virus, HIV, is not spread by casual touching. People can work, play games, and attend school and parties with people who have AIDS without getting the disease.

Bacteria. Other very small microbes make up a group called **bacteria.** (A single microbe of this kind is a *bacterium.*) A line of 1,000 bacteria could fit inside the period at the end of this sentence. The pictures show the different shapes of bacteria.

Bacteria are living cells. Like all living cells, bacteria need food and water to stay alive. Some bacteria need oxygen to live. Others can live where there is no oxygen.

When bacteria can meet their needs to stay alive, they grow. When one bacterium has grown to a certain size, it can divide into two cells. Then the two new cells grow and divide. They become four cells, and then the four become eight cells, and so on.

Most bacteria do not harm people. But if several of the same kind of bacteria grow in your body, an infection can develop. One kind of bacteria can cause a sore throat. Another kind of bacteria can cause an earache.

When bacteria cause an infection, you may get a fever. A **fever** is a body temperature that is higher than normal. When you have a fever, your skin may feel very warm to the touch. A fever is a useful reaction of the body. It can be an early warning sign that you are ill. A fever can slow the growth of disease microbes.

■ *Bacteria that cause strep throat are round. Other bacteria are rods or spirals.*

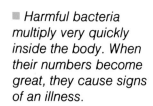

■ *Harmful bacteria multiply very quickly inside the body. When their numbers become great, they cause signs of an illness.*

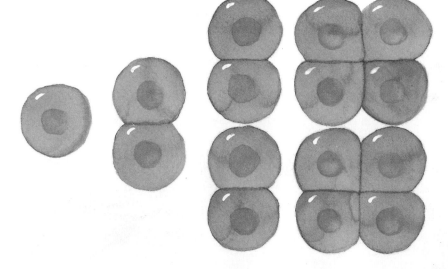

High fever, however, does more harm than good. It causes chills and weakness. It may take you longer to get better if you have an illness with a high fever.

Fungi. Microbes that live and grow like tiny plants are called **fungi.** (A single microbe of this kind is a *fungus.*) Fungi cannot move by themselves. They have to be carried by air, water, and even people. If fungi land in the right place, they can grow and multiply.

Many fungi often live together in large groups. Fungi do not need light in order to live. Some fungi grow best in warm, wet places. Others grow best in cool, dry places. Some fungi grow on or in the human body.

One fungus infection in the mouth is called *thrush.* *Athlete's foot* is a fungus infection of the skin between the toes. *Ringworm* is a skin infection caused by a kind of fungus, not a worm. Ringworm makes a circle-shaped patch, or "ring," where the fungi have infected the skin.

CHECK IT OUT!

In what ways might fungi affect your health? Find out by reading the article on pages B88–91 in the Find Out Resource Center.

SOME HUMAN DISEASES CAUSED BY MICROBES	
Microbes	**Diseases**
Viruses	AIDS chicken pox colds influenza (flu) measles
Bacteria	boils earache sore throat strep throat whooping cough (pertussis)
Fungi	athlete's foot ringworm thrush

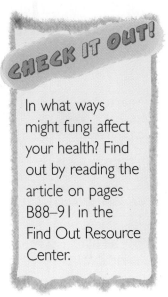
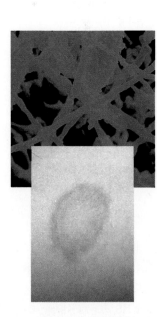

■ *Ringworm, bottom, is a skin disease caused by fungi, top. Ringworm is not caused by worms.*

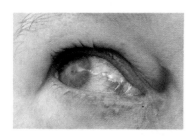

 Neil's eye is infected. The infection is called pinkeye. It can easily spread to other people.

Project checkup

How can this information be included on your bulletin board?

How Can People Prevent Disease?

Having a small number of disease microbes inside your body will usually not harm you. But a greater number of these microbes means a greater chance of becoming ill. Once you have found out how disease microbes are spread, you can take action to keep many of them away from your body. By knowing how microbes spread, you can help others avoid illness.

Neil had an *eye infection*. The infection, called *pinkeye*, was caused by bacteria. His eyes felt itchy, so he rubbed them. The bacteria got on his hands. Then they got on the chalk, the doorknobs, and the other things he touched at school.

Many of Neil's classmates touched those same things. They got pinkeye bacteria on their fingers. Then some of the classmates touched their eyes and faces. In a few days, they had pinkeye as well.

People who are ill can also breathe, sneeze, or cough disease microbes into the air and onto their hands. Then those microbes can get into your eyes, nose, and mouth. This might be the way you got your last cold. It might also be the way you spread your cold to someone else.

Health Skill • Decision Making

It is a warm summer day. Jason and Andrew have been playing in the park for a few hours. Jason is thirsty and wants a drink of water. The water fountains at the park are not working. Jason remembers that a stream runs through the park. Both boys walk to the stream. Andrew tells Jason it is not a good idea to drink from the stream. Jason agrees not to drink the water but wants to rinse his mouth out with it.

? Did Jason make a wise decision? Why or why not? What should the boys do?

Disease microbes can get into different systems of the body. A person might breathe in disease microbes through the respiratory system. Disease microbes might enter the circulatory system through a cut in the skin. A person putting a finger into his or her mouth might be putting disease microbes into the digestive system. Disease microbes can enter adults' bodies through intimate body contact.

If you are ill, you can avoid spreading your disease to others. You can stay home until you are well. You can be careful not to give food to anyone after you have touched it or started to eat it. You can make sure to wash your hands after using the rest room or after covering a cough. You can cover your mouth with a tissue when you cough or sneeze. Then you can put the tissue into the trash so that no one else handles it. You can be careful to keep your mouth off the drinking fountain spout. Tell your teacher if the fountain does not arch the water high enough for you to drink without touching the spout.

How Can You Avoid Disease Microbes?

Disease microbes are everywhere. You can avoid many diseases by drinking water that you know is safe. Ask an adult family member if your water at home comes from a community system or a well. The disease microbes in most community water systems have been killed. Health workers in your community can test the safety of water from wells.

Sometimes, disease microbes grow on food. They can cause the food to spoil. Do not eat any food that looks spoiled or smells different from the way it normally does. Some foods have disease microbes or chemicals on them when you buy them. You need to wash fresh fruits and vegetables before you eat them.

■ Using and disposing of tissues properly and washing your hands can stop the spread of some communicable diseases.

Animals, including insects, spread many diseases by biting people or other animals. Some animals, such as dogs, cats, and squirrels, can spread rabies. Rabies is a dangerous disease that can be spread by animal bites. If any animal ever bites you, tell a parent or another adult at once. Wash the wound with soap and water. You may need to see a physician right away.

Houseflies do not bite, but they are often covered with microbes. Try not to let flies land on your food or on anything else that you might put into your mouth.

REFLECT

Information Check

1. What is the difference between a communicable disease and a noncommunicable disease?
2. What needs to happen in your body before an infection caused by bacteria can occur?

Solving Problems

3. Autumn seems to be getting pinkeye often. What should Autumn do to help herself avoid this communicable disease?

Setting Goals

4. What might you and your classmates do to prevent the spread of some communicable diseases at school as well as at home?

■ *Bacteria can live in the soil, so you need to wash fresh fruits and vegetables before eating them.*

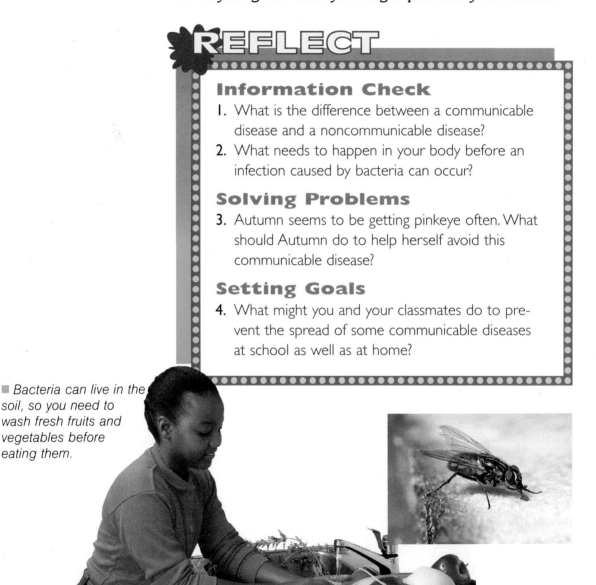

B58

LESSON 2

Fighting Communicable and Noncommunicable Disease

Brandon, Heather, and Carter are classmates. They are friends, too. They play together after school and on most weekends. One day Carter was not at school. Mr. Thomas, their teacher, told the class that Carter was ill with chicken pox. "Chicken pox is a communicable disease caused by a virus," Mr. Thomas said.

Two weeks later, Heather became ill with chicken pox. As more weeks passed, other children in Mr. Thomas's class became ill, too. Brandon, however, did not get chicken pox. Why, do you think, did Brandon not become ill?

How Does Your Body Defend Itself Against Disease?

Your body has ways to defend itself against disease microbes. If these microbes enter your blood, your body's inner defenses go to work. **Immunity** is your body's ability to defend itself against certain kinds of microbes. You become immune to one disease at a time.

FIND OUT

What can I do to protect myself from disease?

▶ Interview a nurse or a physician about disease prevention.
▶ Refer to Unit A, pages A81–87, which discuss health care products.
▶ Refer to pages B23–43, which discuss exercise, rest, and sleep.
▶ Explore the activities and gather information from pages B59–67.

■ A disease such as chicken pox can affect many students in the same class.

B59

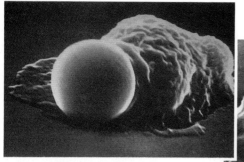
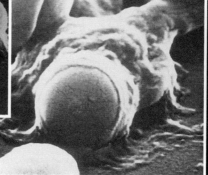
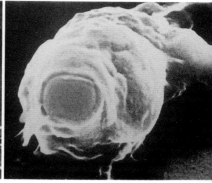

■ *This white blood cell is fighting disease by destroying a disease microbe.*

SOCIAL STUDIES *connection*

SICK DAYS

On Your Own • Since everybody becomes ill at one time or another, businesses and even schools have established certain rules to deal with absences. How does your school handle absences related to illness? Talk to your teacher or someone in your school's attendance office. Share with your classmates what you find out.

Your body's immunity depends partly on your white blood cells. White blood cells are always present in your blood. They work to destroy disease microbes before the microbes can make you ill. If you get an infection, your body makes more white blood cells. They move in your blood to the part of your body that is infected.

Sometimes disease microbes enter your body, and your white blood cells, working alone, cannot destroy them. When this happens, your body uses another defense against disease microbes. This defense uses antibodies. **Antibodies** are chemicals that help defend the body against certain diseases.

Antibodies work with one kind of white blood cell to destroy disease microbes. The antibodies cling to the disease microbes. Then the antibodies send out signals to a certain kind of white blood cell. Those white blood cells then surround and destroy the disease microbes.

Each antibody acts against only one kind of disease microbe. It cannot act against any other kind. For example, if you have chicken pox, your white blood cells will make antibodies just for the chicken-pox virus. These antibodies can cling only to the chicken-pox virus. They can also protect you from the chicken-pox virus for the rest of your life.

After you are well, some of the antibodies stay in your blood. Months or years later, disease microbes of the same kind may enter your body again. This time your body will be prepared. It already has the antibodies needed to stop an infection. You will have immunity to the disease caused by those microbes.

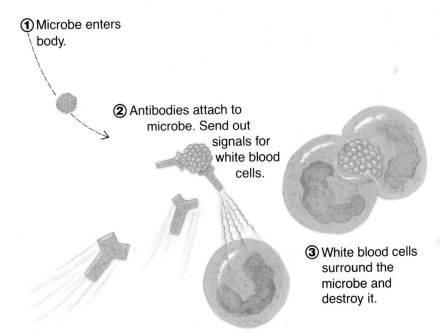

① Microbe enters body.

② Antibodies attach to microbe. Send out signals for white blood cells.

③ White blood cells surround the microbe and destroy it.

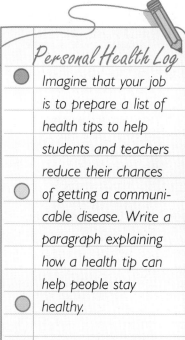
■ *Antibodies are always at work destroying harmful microbes that enter your body.*

What Can You Do to Build Up Your Body's Defenses Against Disease?

Substances called **vaccines** can help you form immunity to some communicable diseases without your having the disease itself. The vaccine against polio is swallowed. Other vaccines are given as *injections,* or "shots."

Each vaccine will protect you from only one disease. For example, you need one kind of vaccine for polio, another kind for measles, and still another kind for mumps. However, two or three kinds of vaccines may be given together in one injection. There are no vaccines yet for some diseases, such as AIDS or colds. A chicken-pox vaccine has been made, but it is not yet widely used.

Personal Health Log

Imagine that your job is to prepare a list of health tips to help students and teachers reduce their chances of getting a communicable disease. Write a paragraph explaining how a health tip can help people stay healthy.

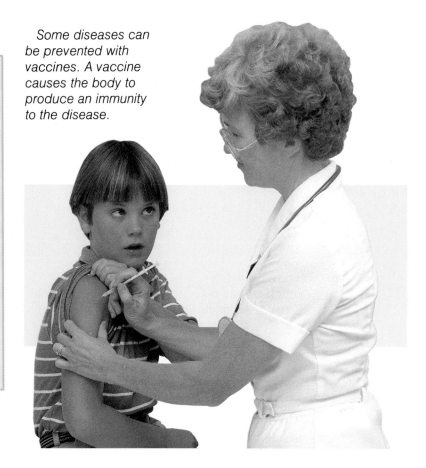

Some diseases can be prevented with vaccines. A vaccine causes the body to produce an immunity to the disease.

Some vaccines can give you immunity to a disease all your life. Others give you immunity for a shorter time. You will need a *booster* of those vaccines. That is, your physician will have to give you the vaccine again in a few years. More vaccine will be needed to boost your immunity, which may have become weak by that time.

Vaccines have been made only for certain diseases. But your body can fight against all diseases better if it has resistance. **Resistance** is the ability of your body to fight disease microbes by itself.

Good health habits can help you build your resistance. You need a balanced diet and plenty of water each day. You also need exercise and enough sleep to feel healthy every day. If you have good health habits, you may avoid getting some diseases. You are taking responsibility for staying healthy.

SCIENCE connection

DISEASE DETECTIVE

On Your Own • Play "disease detective" for a day. Watch for ways you might be spreading disease microbes to others. Have your family members watch themselves, too. At the end of the day, make a list with your family of all the ways you could have spread disease to one another. Then decide what you can do to prevent disease microbes from spreading to others.

Personal Health Log

Are You Doing All You Can to Stop the Spread of Colds?

At the top of a sheet of paper, write the title "How I Can Help Stop the Spread of Colds." Divide the page into four columns, and write the following headings at the tops of the columns. Under each heading, follow the instructions given.

1. ACTIONS I MUST TAKE. List the actions you need to take to meet your goal of stopping the spread of colds.
2. PROBLEMS I MAY FACE. List the things that might interfere with each action you plan to take.
3. HOW TO HANDLE PROBLEMS. List the ways you might handle the problems you may face in each action you plan to take.

4. WHO CAN HELP ME. List people who might help you handle the problems you may face in each action you plan to take.

Try the ideas you have listed to meet your goal of helping stop the spread of communicable disease.

How I Can Help Stop the Spread of Colds			
ACTIONS I MUST TAKE	PROBLEMS I MAY FACE	HOW TO HANDLE PROBLEMS	WHO CAN HELP ME

What Are the Dangers of Heart Diseases and Disorders?

There are many kinds of noncommunicable diseases. There are also noncommunicable health problems that are not diseases. They are called **disorders.** Some disorders, such as being blind, may appear at birth. Other disorders may not affect people until sometime later in their lives. Noncommunicable health problems do not spread from one person to another.

Heart diseases kill more adults in the United States than any other noncommunicable disease. Some people are more likely than others to have heart diseases. High blood pressure and too much fat in the blood may lead to one kind of heart disease. Scientists believe that certain poor health habits also lead to other heart diseases.

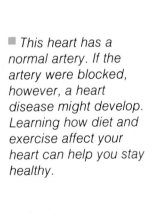

■ This heart has a normal artery. If the artery were blocked, however, a heart disease might develop. Learning how diet and exercise affect your heart can help you stay healthy.

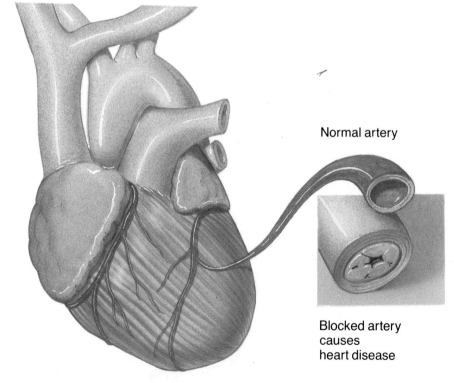

Normal artery

Blocked artery causes heart disease

Heart diseases often take a long time to appear. Sometimes these diseases appear sooner because of poor health habits. Certain health habits also add to the chances of getting a heart disease. People who smoke cigarettes, for example, are more likely to get a heart disease than those who do not smoke. People who eat a high-fat diet or do not exercise enough are also more likely to get a heart disease.

Some people are born with heart disorders. A heart murmur may be a sign of a heart disorder. A *heart murmur* is a sound that is not usually made by a healthy heart. The sound may be made by a heart valve that does not close tightly. Many heart murmurs in children are just normal sounds for a young heart.

What Is Cancer?

Cancer is a kind of noncommunicable disease that can damage any part of the body. Nearly half a million people in the United States die from cancer each year. Many people who have cancer can be treated for it. If cancer is treated early, the person may get well again.

There are about two hundred different kinds of cancer. All kinds of cancer begin with one harmful cell. Scientists are not sure why cancer cells start to grow. Cancer cells grow faster and divide sooner than healthy cells. Cancer cells form lumps. These lumps then grow in place of other healthy cells. Cancer cells keep a healthy cell from working. Not all body lumps are signs of cancer. All lumps need to be checked by a physician.

Cancer can grow in people of any age. But some people are more likely to get cancer than other people. Sometimes several members of one family will get a certain cancer. People who use tobacco products are much more likely to get cancer of the mouth, throat, or lungs than people who do not. People who work with certain chemicals risk getting certain kinds of cancer.

CHECK IT OUT!

What can you do to keep from getting heart diseases? You can find out by contacting your local chapter of the American Heart Association (see pages B98–99 of the Find Out Resource Center). Refer also to pages B13–19, which discuss wise food choices for wellness.

■ *Special clothing can protect workers from cancer-causing materials.*

■ *Using a sunscreen protects your skin and may prevent certain kinds of skin cancer.*

CHECK IT OUT!

Why is skin cancer one of the most common kinds of cancer? Find out more about its causes and symptoms, and learn how to prevent it. Your school librarian can help you find books or magazines on the subject. Also refer to "Talking with a Cancer Researcher" on page B78.

Project checkup

What information about skin cancer will you include on your bulletin board?

Some kinds of cancer are easy to prevent. Skin cancer, for example, is caused by getting too much sun. Being responsible for your health by protecting your skin from the sun may help you prevent skin cancer.

What Are Allergies?

One kind of disorder many people have is an allergy. An **allergy** is a noncommunicable disorder in which a person is bothered by a certain thing, such as dust, tiny parts of plants, insect stings, animal hair, or certain foods or chemicals. Something that causes an allergic reaction in a person may not bother most other people. An allergy can come about at any age. The symptoms of an allergy may happen at any time.

Hay fever is really an allergy. Some people are allergic to tiny parts of plants. The parts float in the air. A person with hay fever will have symptoms after

■ *Some people are allergic to certain foods or certain kinds of cloth.*

■ *Poison ivy is a plant that causes allergy symptoms in most people.*

breathing in those tiny parts. Some symptoms are sneezing, red eyes, and a runny nose. People with hay fever or other allergies can be treated by a physician. A physician can order medicines to help ease the symptoms of hay fever.

A rash from poison ivy is really an allergy symptom. It is not poisoning. A person who has an allergy to the poison ivy plant can have a rash. A physician may need to help the person if the rash does not go away in a few days.

REFLECT

Information Check
1. What is immunity?
2. How do antibodies work to protect your health?
3. What are two possible causes of heart diseases?

Solving Problems
4. Than's classmates are catching colds. What can Than do to avoid catching a cold or spreading a cold to his family and friends?

Setting Goals
5. How do you plan to protect yourself from communicable diseases?

SHARE

You have gathered a lot of information about guarding against disease. Think of ways you can share something you have learned with others. Here are some ideas:

▶ Show your disease prevention bulletin board to other classes.

▶ Work with your classmates as a team to provide others in your school with information about diseases and disease prevention.

▶ Direct other students interested in information about diseases and disease prevention to places where they too can find important facts and information.

ACT

Health is more than gathering information—it is making wise choices and practicing good health habits. How might you use what you have learned about guarding against disease? Here are some things you can do for . . .

Yourself

▶ Find out if your vaccinations are complete and up to date.

▶ Plan how you can avoid infections and diseases.

Your Family

▶ Talk with your family about what you have learned and how this information can benefit everyone's health.

Your School and Community

▶ See what kinds of programs your local health department has available for disease prevention.

What will you do?

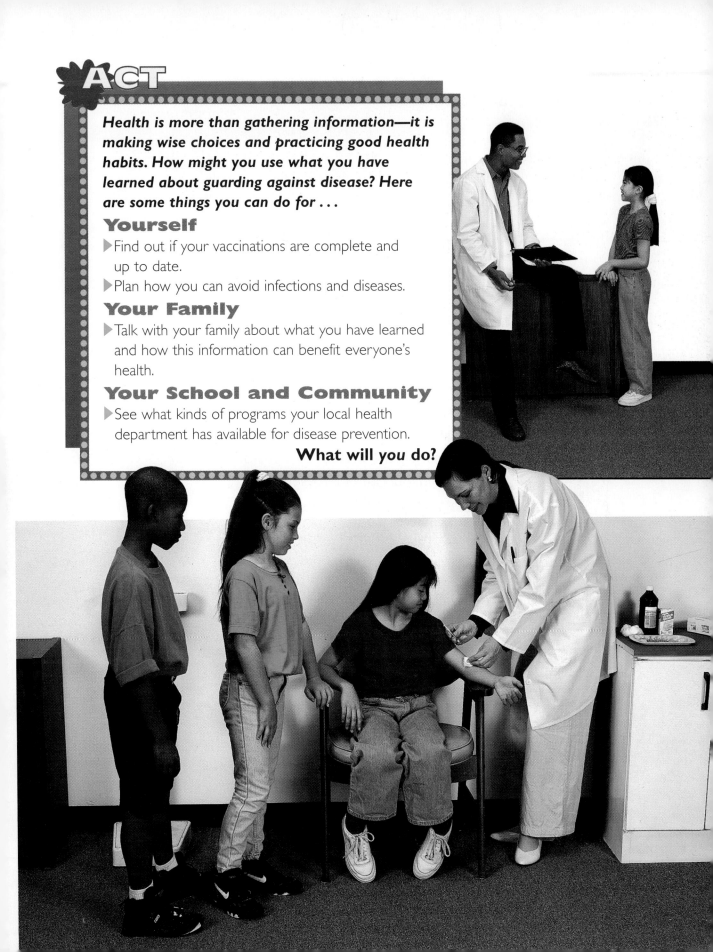

Find Out!

There are many sources that can help you find answers to your health questions. Use this Resource Center to help you gather information.

Find Out . . .

Resource Center

Find Out

from People

You can often get answers to your questions on a topic from people who work in that field. Ask an adult family member to help you contact a person of your choice. Some ideas are provided below.

In the articles on pages B74–79, you can read about other people who work in health-related fields.

PEOPLE TO CONTACT

An Exercise Instructor .

An exercise instructor is a person who plans and directs exercise programs for other people. Exercise instructors design programs that will increase endurance, flexibility, and muscle strength.

A Food Scientist. . . . . .

A food scientist is a trained person whose goal is to provide a safe, nutritious, and plentiful food supply for people. Food scientists work in research laboratories, teach at colleges and universities, and also work for the government.

A Medical Laboratory Technician . . . .

A medical laboratory technician performs medical tests in medical laboratories and in hospitals. These technicians study tissue and blood samples and test for the presence of diseases.

TIPS FOR CONDUCTING INTERVIEWS in Person or by Telephone

▶ Make a list of the questions you want to ask.

▶ Select a telephone in a quiet location where you will not be disturbed. Have pencil and paper and your list of questions with you.

▶ Call the person you want to interview. Identify yourself and the reason for your call. Make an appointment for the interview, either in person or by phone. Be sure to arrive or call promptly at the appointed time.

▶ During the interview, speak slowly and clearly. Ask the questions you prepared. Take notes as your questions are answered. As the interview continues, you may think of other questions you want to ask.

▶ After you have asked all your prepared questions, ask the person if there is any other information he or she would like to share with you.

▶ Ask the person for the names of groups or organizations that might have information they could send you. Be ready to write down the names, addresses, and phone numbers.

▶ When the interview is complete, thank the person for his or her time and information and say good-bye politely.

An Interview with a
Clinical Dietitian

Stephanie Mullican knows about food and good health. She is a clinical dietitian at a hospital in Orlando, Florida.

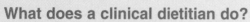

What does a clinical dietitian do?

A clinical dietitian helps people in hospitals. I work as part of a health

■ *A clinical dietitian knows the importance of good nutrition for a healthy body.*

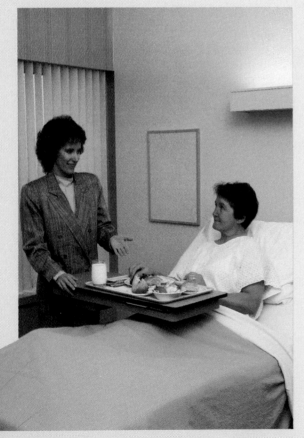

care team to decide on the best nutrition plan for each of the patients.

How would you describe the hardest part of your job?

Teaching about proper diet is the hardest part. Many people in hospitals are not ready to learn about diet. So we take care of their food needs for them. While they are in the hospital, we decide what they may eat. When these people go home, they are on their own. Before they leave the hospital, I visit with them and sometimes with the people who will prepare their meals at home. Teaching people about proper diet means talking about what people eat and how they prepare their food. It may change what the whole family is served.

What is the biggest surprise you have found in your work?

This would be the number of young people I see with high levels of fat in their diets. A great many young people between the ages of 9 and 11 eat a high-fat diet. It is clear to me that they do not have balanced diets. To stay healthy, they need to have a variety of foods each day.

When did you know you wanted to be a dietitian?

I first became interested in nutrition in junior high school. I suppose that

■ *Stephanie Mullican is a clinical dietitian. She tells people that a balanced diet helps keep them healthy.*

was because I was overweight. I am still learning new things about food all the time. I make wiser food choices today than I did in the past.

How did you become a clinical dietitian?

I went to school at Florida State University. Then I worked as a student dietitian at a hospital in South Carolina. My job was to check all the food for the patients. I made sure that the right food went to the right person. After that, I took a national test. To become a registered dietitian, you must pass a test given by the American Dietetic Association. Even after you pass the test, you must keep taking classes. There is always something new to learn.

What subjects did you study in school?

I studied chemistry and biology to learn how the body works. I took classes about nutrition. Because food is bought and sold, I studied business and economics. I also learned how and why people make food choices. I took cooking classes, and I even learned the history of foods and eating habits.

What do you think young people should know about your job?

They should understand that a clinical dietitian is part of a larger health care team. The whole team—which includes physicians, nurses, and others—works together to help people in hospitals. A dietitian knows that it is important to live what you teach. If people are to believe what I tell them, they must see me as a good example for proper nutrition.

Learn more about people who work as dietitians in schools, hospitals, and businesses. Interview a dietitian. Or write for information to the American Dietetic Association, 216 W. Jackson Boulevard, Suite 800, Chicago, IL 60606-6995.

Questions for a
Physical Education Teacher

Karen Kerley knows the importance of exercise. She is a physical education teacher at an elementary school in Schenectady, New York.

What do you do as a physical education teacher?

I teach up to eight physical education classes a day to elementary school students. I begin each class by having students do warm-up exercises. I always tell students what muscles they are warming up. That way they learn where different muscles are. After the warm-ups, I have students complete a lesson. The lesson depends on the activity or sport I am teaching that day. Some of the sports I teach during the year are cross-country running, soccer, touch football, floor hockey, basketball, and tumbling. After students have completed their day's lesson, I have them cool down by doing slower exercises. Near the end of class, I discuss with students what they have learned.

What happens to the body during exercise?

Exercise helps the blood flow faster through the heart and the rest of the body. Because the heart is a muscle,

■ Warming up is an important part of exercise.

■ *Ms. Kerley enjoys teaching students how to improve their physical fitness.*

exercise makes it stronger. After a few weeks of exercise, the heart does not have to work as hard to pump blood. Also, exercise makes the lungs able to hold more air. The faster flow of blood and the greater intake of air mean more oxygen goes to the body's cells faster. Overall, exercise helps students' bodies work more efficiently. That means they do not waste any effort.

How can students tell when their hearts and lungs are not wasting any effort?

If a student puts a hand to his or her chest after exercise, the student will feel that it takes less and less time for the heartbeat to return to normal. On the first day of exercise, it might take two or three minutes for the heart-beat to return to normal. After a few weeks, it may take only 30 seconds. The less time it takes the body's heart-beat and breathing to return to normal, the stronger the body is getting.

What does exercise do for students in addition to making the body fit?

Exercise often helps students build confidence in themselves. When they improve their physical condition, they often improve their self-esteem. When students see that they can practice and improve physically, they realize they can practice and improve in other areas of their lives as well. Some stu-dents will never be the best athletes in class, but at least they know they can get better at something. Also, students learn through sports to cooperate with one another. They learn to share in order to reach a goal.

What do you like most about being a physical education teacher?

I enjoy my job most when students realize that they have improved. Sometimes one student will point out the improvement in another student's skills. At other times, a student might say all of a sudden, "I'm getting better!" Sometimes I can tell students feel they have improved—when I see the smiles on their faces.

*L*earn more about physical education teachers. Interview a physical education teacher. Or write for information to the American Alliance for Health, Physical Education, Recreation, and Dance, 1900 Association Drive, Reston, VA 22091.

Talking with a
Cancer Researcher

Philip A. Pizzo helps children who are ill with cancer. He is a cancer researcher at the National Cancer Institute in Bethesda, Maryland.

What does a cancer researcher do?

A cancer researcher tries to understand cancer. He or she studies why

■ Dr. Pizzo helps young people who have cancer.

cancer happens and what can be done to prevent it and treat it.

How have cancer researchers helped children?

They have helped save the lives of many children. The cancer most often seen in children is called *leukemia.* Leukemia is cancer of the blood cells. Not long ago, most children who had leukemia died as a result of it. Some died as soon as three months after becoming ill. Today, more than half of the children with leukemia are cured. They go on to lead normal lives. This change came about because of cancer research.

How have cancer researchers saved lives?

Cancer researchers have made many different medicines that fight cancer cells. They have also learned how to treat people with these medicines. This kind of treatment is called drug therapy, or *chemotherapy.*

When did you know you wanted to study cancer?

I decided to go into cancer research when I was a young physician. While I worked in a hospital, I was learning about noncommunicable diseases that affect children. I saw children who had cancer. I saw that there was a lot of work to be done. I believed that if I became a cancer researcher, I could help children. I felt I wanted to make things better. I wanted to learn new ways of helping children and bring new ideas to the treatment of cancer.

Besides medicine, did you need to know other things to be a researcher?

Cancer treatment and research call for a lot of knowledge and experience. A researcher needs to know about cancer cells and how they grow. But a researcher needs to know much more than that. I had to learn how to help people face cancer. That means helping not only patients but also their parents, other family members, and friends.

Researchers work in laboratories. What does research have to do with caring for patients?

There are two kinds of research. One is called *basic research*. It is done in laboratories. There researchers look at how cancer cells behave. The second kind of research is called *clinical research*. It is about better ways to treat patients. Both kinds of research really have to do with treating people. For example, it is important to know the effects that different cancer drugs have on children with cancer.

What do you like best about your work?

I feel a great deal of satisfaction when I see a child get better. One of the things I like best is seeing a child get well because of a treatment I

■ *New information from cancer research is important to Dr. Pizzo. He studies cancer research reports so he can help his patients. He helps his patients understand what cancer is and how they can be treated.*

helped develop. I have always been excited by the challenge of helping children get well.

Learn more about people who work as cancer researchers. Interview a researcher. Or write for information to the American Cancer Society, 1599 Clifton Road, N.E., Atlanta, GA 30329-4251.

Find Out

from History

Knowing how scientific discoveries have advanced over the years can help you understand how and why certain things are done today. In the following section, you can find out how our understanding of a healthful diet has changed over time.

Finding the Balanced Diet, Then and Now

One thing that we all have in common is our daily need for food. No one can live without it. However, eating just any food is not necessarily healthful. Scientists tell us that there has to be a balance.

To nourish our bodies and maintain our health, we must eat healthful foods that are part of a balanced diet. People have not always known what makes up a balanced diet. History is full of stories of deficiency diseases that could have been avoided if people had only known the importance of healthful eating.

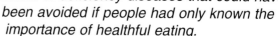

■ Balanced meals are important.

■ *Sailors were once plagued by scurvy.*

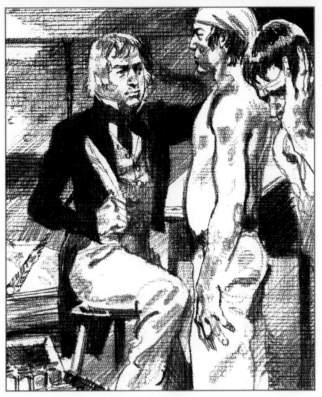

Fruits of Knowledge

Years ago it was common for sailors on long voyages to suffer from a disease called *scurvy*. Scurvy is a disease in which the gums bleed, the teeth become loose, and wounds do not heal. Scurvy was a problem until it was discovered that eating citrus fruits—such as oranges, lemons, and limes—prevented it. Not until years later did scientists discover that scurvy was caused by a diet lacking in vitamin C. The scientists learned that citrus fruits contain vitamin C and that this vitamin helps wounds heal and keeps the teeth and gums firm.

It was found that other diseases, too, were caused by diet deficiencies. For instance, *rickets* is a disease that causes abnormally shaped bones. It was found to be the result of a diet lacking in milk and eggs, which supply the body with vitamin D. *Beriberi* is a disease that affects digestion and muscle movement. This disease was found to be caused by a lack of vitamin B_1. If not diagnosed and corrected, any of these diet-related diseases can result in death.

Food for Thought

Understanding the causes of diseases like scurvy, rickets, and beriberi helped in the prevention and treatment of them. Scientific research also provided a new understanding of food. Scientists began studying foods to determine their nutritional value. Governments began publishing food guidelines for a healthful diet.

Soon, food guidelines became a part of health and science textbooks. As early as the 1940s, these books told about the need for foods that contained the vitamins. By 1955 the U.S. government was publishing a pie-shaped chart displaying the "Basic 7" or "Seven Basic Food Groups." The chart included a variety of foods that would help people maintain a healthful, balanced diet. It even suggested numbers of daily servings needed for the proper amounts of nutrients.

A few years later, the chart was changed. Some of the food groups were combined, reducing the seven food groups to four. The new chart was referred to as the "Four Basic Food Groups." These food groups were (1) meat, poultry, fish, and eggs; (2) milk and milk products; (3) vegetables and fruits; and (4) bread and other flour products. This chart served as a nutritional guide until the 1990s.

The Seven Basic Food Groups became the Four Basic Food Groups.

■ *The USDA felt the Food Guide Pyramid was a better way to show foods for a healthful diet.*

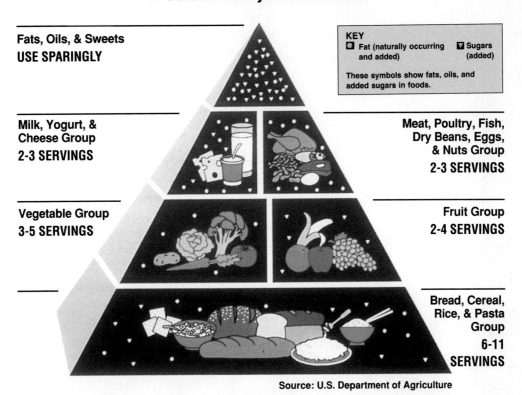

Food Guide Pyramid
A Guide to Daily Food Choices

**Fats, Oils, & Sweets
USE SPARINGLY**

KEY
□ Fat (naturally occurring and added) ▼ Sugars (added)

These symbols show fats, oils, and added sugars in foods.

**Milk, Yogurt, & Cheese Group
2-3 SERVINGS**

**Meat, Poultry, Fish, Dry Beans, Eggs, & Nuts Group
2-3 SERVINGS**

**Vegetable Group
3-5 SERVINGS**

**Fruit Group
2-4 SERVINGS**

**Bread, Cereal, Rice, & Pasta Group
6-11 SERVINGS**

Source: U.S. Department of Agriculture

The Food Guide Pyramid

The newest food guide is not in the form of a chart. The U.S. Department of Agriculture (USDA) chose a pyramid instead. The USDA felt that the "Food Guide Pyramid" was a better way to show the foods and the amounts needed for a healthful diet. Agriculture Secretary Edward R. Madigan said, "The new graphic conveys the three essential elements of a healthy diet: proportion, moderation, and variety."

The food pyramid shows bread and grain foods at the base and fruits and vegetables on the next level. Meat and dairy foods are on the third level, with high-fat and sugary foods topping the pyramid.

Like the food guides before it, the Food Guide Pyramid is the result of research on nutrition. As the years go by, people will continue to learn more about the foods that make up a healthful diet. Maybe our view of a healthful diet will change again in the years to come.

Find Out

from Articles

Magazines, brochures, and newspapers often contain interesting articles about new developments and ideas in health. The following articles contain information about diet, snack foods, and disease-causing organisms.

Guidelines

for a Healthful Diet

- Eat a variety of healthful foods from the following food groups:
  - Bread, Cereal, Rice, and Pasta Group
  - Vegetable Group
  - Fruit Group
  - Milk, Yogurt, and Cheese Group
  - Meat, Poultry, Fish, Dry Beans, Eggs, and Nuts Group
- Eat few foods that are high in fat content, such as deep-fried foods, butter and other fat-rich dairy products, and red meat.

- Eat whole-grain products, vegetables, and fruits. Foods such as whole-grain breads, cereals, potatoes, and fresh vegetables and fruits are high in complex carbohydrates and fiber. Carbohydrates should represent about one-half of your daily calories.
- Achieve and maintain your ideal body weight. You may become overweight by eating more calories than your body uses. You can reduce your weight by eating fewer calories and less fat and by exercising more.
- Limit the amount of sweets that you eat. These foods are high in calories but provide very few nutrients.
- Avoid using additional salt, or sodium, in your diet. Limit your use of the salt-shaker, and reduce your intake of foods such as pretzels, salted crackers, dill pickles, and cured or smoked meats.
- Drink plenty of water. Your body needs a ready supply of water to help transport nutrients, eliminate wastes, and regulate body temperature.

Food Needs of Young People 9 to 12 Years of Age

Food Group	Recommended Daily Amounts	Average Serving
Bread, Cereal Rice, and Pasta	6–11 servings	1 slice bread 1 ounce dry cereal 1/2 cup cooked cereal, rice, or pasta
Vegetable	3–5 servings	1 cup raw, leafy vegetables 1/2 cup cooked or chopped raw vegetables 3/4 cup vegetable juice
Fruit	2–4 servings	1 medium-sized apple, banana, or orange 1/2 cup chopped, cooked, or canned fruit 3/4 cup fruit juice
Milk, Yogurt, and Cheese	2–3 servings	1 cup milk or yogurt 1 1/2 ounces natural cheese 2 ounces processed cheese
Meat, Poultry, Fish, Dry Beans, Eggs, and Nuts	2–3 servings	2–3 ounces cooked lean meat, poultry, or fish 1/2 cup cooked dry beans, 1 egg, or 2 tablespoons peanut butter count as 1 ounce lean meat

Healthful Snacks

Your health and growth depend greatly on the foods you eat. Therefore, you should try to eat the most nutritious and healthful foods that you can. This applies whether you are eating a formal meal or just having a snack. Unfortunately, many of the foods that are often eaten as snacks are not very healthful. They contain many calories and few or no nutrients. The foods listed here will help you to "snack smart." These foods are easy to find, nutritious, and taste great!

Crunchies

Apples and pears

Broccoli spears

Carrot and celery sticks

Cauliflower chunks

Green-pepper sticks

Radishes

Unsalted rice cakes

Zucchini slices

Hot Stuff

Soups: clear soups, homemade vegetable or tomato soups

Cocoa made with nonfat milk

Tortillas topped with green chilies and a little grated mozzarella

Munchies

Almonds and walnuts

Bagels

Bread sticks

Popcorn (prepared without butter, margarine, oil, or salt)

Mixture of 2 cups soy nuts, 2 cups raw peanuts roasted in oven, and 1 cup raisins or other dried fruit

Mozzarella (made from part-skim milk)

Unsalted sunflower seeds

Whole-grain breads

Sweet Stuff

Baked apple (plain—without sugar or pastry)

Dried fruit

Fresh fruit

Raisins

Thin slice of angel food cake

Unsweetened canned fruit

Thirst Quenchers

Nonfat milk or buttermilk

Unsweetened juices

Unsweetened fruit juice concentrate mixed with club soda

FUNGUS Among Us

from *Current Health 1*

One mushroom says to another mushroom, "I don't know what's wrong with me. I can't get a date. I just don't understand it. I'm a fungi (fun guy)!"

Fun Guy or Fungi?

Desmond Layton couldn't stand it anymore. He pulled off his shoes, yanked away his socks, and scratched his itching feet. Then he noticed the scaly, cracked, soggy skin between his toes.

Mr. Layton looked at his son's feet and said, "ATHLETE'S FOOT." Desmond thought that sounded like a good problem to have, but his feet smelled terrible and itched like mad.

The next day, Dr. Wymie told Desmond that he had a form of *ringworm*.

The boy raised his eyebrows. "Ringworm? Worms in my feet?"

"No, Desmond," the doctor smiled. "This is not worms like earthworms. Ringworm is a *microorganism* (mī-krō-or´-gun-izm), a kind of fungi."

■ Athlete's foot fungus

"I'm a fun guy."

"I'm sure you are, but ringworm is a fungus or fungi (the plural of fungus) that lives on the outer layers of skin, nails, and hair."

"Fungus? You mean like the fuzzy stuff that grows on fruit or the green gunk on old bread?"

"Yes. Mold is a type of fungi. A fungus cannot make its own food. Some fungi are *parasites* (pair´- ə -sīts), which live off living things. Others are *saprophytes* (sap´rə -fīts), which live off dead things. Some fungi grow as molds on food as you said. Others live on the skin of humans.

"There's ringworm of the scalp, . . ."

Desmond touched his head.

". . .body ringworm, . . ."

He suddenly felt hot.

". . .and many other forms of the fungus, including the kind known as athlete's foot."

Desmond grinned. "I play soccer, basketball, and baseball."

"Great," the doctor nodded. "But you don't have to be an athlete to get athlete's foot."

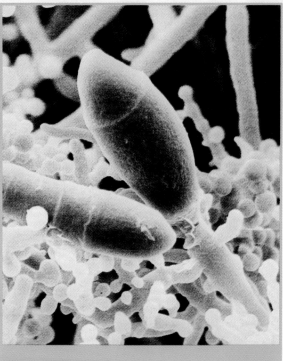

The most important thing is to keep your body clean and dry.

Not for Athletes Only

"So who gets it?" Desmond asked, confused.

He was told that athlete's foot is common during the teen years, especially among boys. People used to think that the fungus was picked up in places where athletes were likely to be found (like swimming pools), but scientists have found fungi almost everywhere.

The most likely explanation for the cause of athlete's foot is the fact that we wear shoes most of the time. The three things that all fungi need are warmth, dampness, and oxygen. Since shoes keep the feet warm and can cause sweating and redness, especially between the toes, feet are perfect places for fungi to thrive.

"In fact," said the doctor, "athlete's foot is not seen in countries where people go barefoot most of the time or wear sandals."

Desmond nodded, scratching. "So how do you get it other places?" he asked.

"You know, Desmond, ringworm of the scalp isn't itchy like athlete's foot, but it does cause scaling and patches of baldness. You can get it from another infected person through things like using the person's combs, hairbrushes, and hats. All you

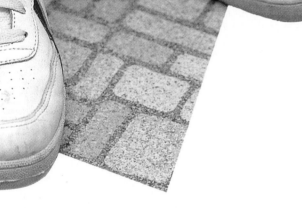

■ *Shoes can promote the growth of athlete's foot.*

ringworm can be spread from floors, shower stalls, benches, or anything the fungi can live on."

Fungus Busters

The doctor told Desmond that athlete's foot is easy to treat. "In fact, in mild cases like yours, it's often not even necessary to go to a doctor. Your toes should be dried very carefully after bathing or after taking off your shoes. It's best to do this with a dry washcloth, rubbing just hard enough to remove the soggy skin and scales. Keep your feet dry: Air them out, sprinkle on absorbent powder, and when you go out, try to wear ventilated shoes or, in warm weather, sandals.

"The most important thing, Desmond, is to keep your body clean and dry. That will help keep ringworm problems from

need is a minor bruise of the scalp, and you have an entryway for the infection."

"And what about my body?"

"Body ringworm is common on the face, arms, and shoulders of boys and girls—and on the groin of teenage boys, it is often called 'jock itch.' It usually starts as a flat, red spot. It then gets bigger and takes a horseshoe shape, with blisters on the outer rim and a peeling center. Body

returning. Dust your toes with powder when you get up in the morning and other times during the day when you take off your shoes. If you sweat a lot, change your socks more than once a day. Also, don't use other people's hairbrushes or combs, don't share your clothes—and keep your hat on your own head. OK?"

An absorbent powder can help keep feet dry.

On his way home, Desmond reviewed what he learned: Ringworm is a fungus. It is not a worm and does not form rings. And athlete's foot is a form of ringworm, but you don't have to be an athlete to get it. And though it's a kind of fungi, there's nothing fun about it.

Find Out

from Books

Many interesting fiction and nonfiction books have been written on health-related topics. You may enjoy reading some of the following books that can be found in your school media center or a local library.

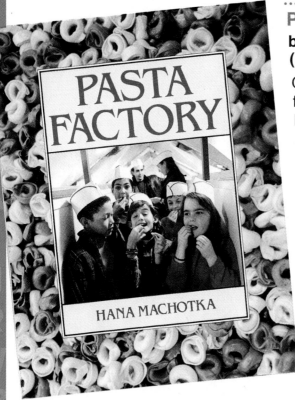

Pasta Factory
by Hana Machotka (Houghton Mifflin, 1992).

Go on a field trip to a pasta factory! That's right. In this book, you can join a group of students as they tour the Tutta Pasta Factory in New York City. As you read, you will discover how the ever-popular pasta is made.

Rice: The Little Grain That Feeds the World
by Raphaëlle Brice (Young Discovery Library, 1991).

Is rice a part of your daily diet? It is for millions of people. Read and see for yourself how this tiny grain has fed people for centuries. This fascinating book looks at how rice is grown and at its importance as a food and for other uses.

Allergies—What They Are, What They Do

**by Judith S. Seixas
(Greenwillow, 1991).**

Do you have any allergies? Perhaps you have a friend who has to cope with an allergy. Now you can have a better understanding of allergies. This book outlines the various allergy symptoms and describes ways to treat them.

Carlos and the Squash Plant

**by Jan Romero Stevens
(Northland, 1993).**

Carlos enjoys tilling the rich brown earth on his parents' farm in northern New Mexico, but his dislike of baths leads him to ignore his mother's warnings about what will happen if he doesn't wash the dirt out of his ears. What a surprise Carlos gets when the itching in his right ear turns out to be a sprouting plant that grows longer and longer and gets more and more difficult to fit under his hat!

Rabies

**by Elaine Landau
(Dutton, 1993).**

What is rabies? Why do you need to protect your pets from rabies? The

rabies virus is a deadly threat to animals and people. Find out how rabies is spread and how you can protect your pets and yourself.

Alex, the Kid with AIDS

**by Linda Walvoord Girard
(Albert Whitman, 1991).**

Alex is a fourth-grader with AIDS. He is also the new kid in class. Discover how Alex makes a new friend and learns that although he is sick he can't misbehave in school.

Find Out

from Multimedia Resources

On-line Services

On-line services can bring you up-to-date on the latest discoveries. They can help you get information on health-related topics from people all over the country.

Classroom Prodigy

Prodigy Services Company
445 Hamilton Avenue
White Plains, NY 10601
1-800-776-3449
Offers curriculum-oriented content, communications features, and classroom-to-classroom activities.

The Free Educational Mail Network

FrEdMail Foundation
P.O. Box 243
Bonita, CA 91908
(619) 475-4852
The oldest and largest educational network in the United States. Uses the Internet to link more than 150 electronic bulletin boards operated by individuals and institutions.
Network Connection: *Internet arogers@bonita.cerf.fred.org*

Scholastic Network

730 Broadway
New York, NY 10003
Provides access to online encyclopedias, the major news wires, *Scholastic* magazines, and other educational materials.
Network Connection: *America Online Network*

National Geographic Kids Network

National Geographic Society
Educational Services
P.O. Box 96892
Washington, D.C. 20090
1-800-368-2728
International telecommunications-based curriculum in which students conduct research, compile data, and share findings with teammates across the United States and around the world. Topics for investigation include acid rain, pollution, and nutrition.
Network Connection: *National Geographic Network*

Computer Software

Many computer programs have information and activities about health-related topics. Here are some possibilities you can investigate. A media specialist can help you find more.

"Let's Eat!" Discovering Facts About Food

Cambridge Development Laboratory, Inc.
86 West Street
Waltham, MA 02154
Eating healthy meals can now be more fun as you begin to explore the health facts with this computer program!

Food for Thought

Cambridge Development Laboratory, Inc.
86 West Street
Waltham, MA 02154
What kinds of food does your body need each day in order for you to remain healthy? Explore good nutrition with this software.

You Are What You Eat

Cambridge Development Laboratory, Inc.
86 West Street
Waltham, MA 02154
How are you doing at making choices for healthful foods? Plug in the information about your diet and find out!

Nutrition Nabber

Educational Software Institute
4213 South 94th Street
Omaha, NE 68127
Test your skill at identifying nutritious foods. See if you can identify the food that has the greatest amount of a nutrient. Play the game and find out more about nutrition.

Video Media

Videotapes, videodiscs, and films can provide interesting information about health care and related topics. Here are some videos that you may enjoy viewing with your classmates.

Posture

Agency for Instructional Technology
Box A
Bloomington, IN 47402-0120
Improve your posture and muscle efficiency with the exercises presented in this video.

Fitness

Agency for Instructional Technology
Box A
Bloomington, IN 47402-0120
There are many different ways of being fit. Find out where you "fit" in.

More Food

TVOntario/USA
1140 Kildaire Farm Road, Suite 308
Cary, NC 27511
Why is eating well important for you? Watch this video and find out.

Find Out

from Places to Visit

Many institutions, offices, and organizations will allow you to visit and tour their facilities. Here are some places you might visit to gather information. Use the tips below to prepare for your visit and to report your findings to friends and family members when you return.

GETTING THE MOST FROM A FIELD TRIP

- Choose a place to visit, either from the suggestions given or from one of your own ideas.

- Prepare questions about the functions of or work done at the facility.

- Prepare a sheet of paper on which to record the information you receive during a field trip.

- Call the facility to find out whether student tours are given. Obtain the names of the person who can give permission for the tour and the person who will guide the tour.

- Arrange the time and date of the visit or the tour of the facility. Be sure to arrive promptly at the appointed time.

- Take notes as you tour or observe the workings of the facility. Be sure to include people you meet, such as directors, guides, and technicians, but do not include other visitors.

- You may wish to take photographs of the facility while you are visiting, but be sure to obtain permission before taking them.

- When your visit is complete, review your notes and write a report on what you learned at the facility. You may want to include as part of your report any photographs you have taken as well as literature, such as brochures, you obtained during your visit.

A Gymnasium

A gymnasium is a center in a community where people can go to participate in physical activities.

Visit a gymnasium near you and talk with an exercise instructor. Ask him or her to tell you about the classes that are provided.

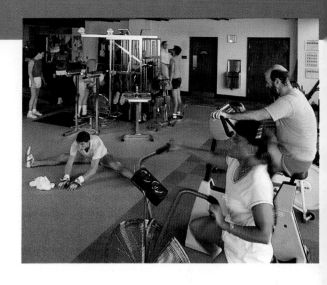

A University Research Lab

Universities often have research laboratories. These facilities enable college students and scientists to do research work.

Contact a local university and see whether scientists there are doing any food research. Talk with a scientist and see if he or she can give you a tour.

A Hospital Medical Lab

Hospitals maintain medical laboratory facilities. These facilities provide physicians with test results and medical analyses for the treatment of patients.

Arrange a tour of a medical laboratory, and interview one of the technicians. Ask him or her to explain how technicians do their work.

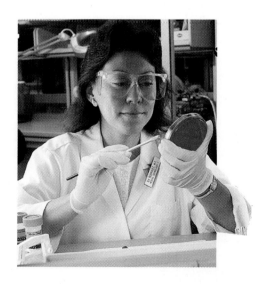

Find Out

from Organizations

Many organizations can be contacted by letter or telephone to answer your questions. Use the tips on the next page when preparing your letters or refer to the tips on page B73 when calling for information.

Directory of Health Services and Agencies

American Academy of Pediatrics
141 Northwest Point Boulevard
P.O. Box 927
Elk Grove Village, IL 60009
(708) 228-5005
Sends pamphlets; public education staff answers questions.

American Alliance for Health, Physical Education, Recreation and Dance
1900 Association Drive
Reston, VA 22091
(703) 476-3400
Provides periodicals and special publications.

American Anorexia/Bulimia Association, Inc.
418 East 76th Street
New York, NY 10021
(212) 891-8686
Provides referral service and mails information.

American Heart Association
1150 Connecticut Avenue, N.W.
Suite 810
Washington, DC 20036
(202) 822-9380
(800) AHA USA1
Conducts research and education on heart disease.

American Kidney Fund
6110 Executive Boulevard
Suite 1010
Rockville, MD 20852
(301) 881-3052
(800) 638-8299
Provides information and financial assistance to kidney patients.

American Red Cross National Headquarters
430 17th Street, N.W.
Washington, DC 20006
(202) 737-8300
Publishes booklets and other materials and offers various services.

American School Health Association
7263 State Route 43
P.O. Box 708
Kent, OH 44240
(216) 678-1601
Publishes magazines and newsletters; has catalog of other publications.

Anorexia Bulimia Treatment and Education Center
Mercy Center for Eating Disorders
301 St. Paul Place
Baltimore, MD 21202
(410) 332-9800
Answers questions and provides material on the disorders.

Centers for Disease Control
1600 Clifton Road, N.E.
Atlanta, GA 30333
(404) 639-3311
Publishes weekly and monthly reports on diseases.

Consumer Information Center
18th and F Streets, N.W.
Washington, DC 20405
(202) 501-1794
Supplies free or minimal-cost pamphlets on topics of consumer interest.

Council of Better Business Bureaus
4200 Wilson Boulevard
Suite 800
Arlington, VA 22203
(703) 276-0100

Provides information on nonprofit organizations and publishes low-cost pamphlets.

Food and Drug Administration (FDA)
Office of Consumer Affairs
Public Inquiries
5600 Fishers Lane (HFE-88)
Rockville, MD 20857
(301) 443-3170
Provides free publications on food, drugs, cosmetics, and food labeling.

Kidsnet
6856 Eastern Avenue N.W., Suite 208
Washington, DC 20012
(202) 291-1400
Sends information geared to 6- to 12-year-olds on AIDS, food labeling, and other topics.

National Center for Missing and Exploited Children
2101 Wilson Boulevard, Suite 550
Arlington, VA 22201
(800) 843-5678
Publishes brochures and books.

National Health Information Clearinghouse
P.O. Box 1133
Washington, DC 20013-1133
(800) 336-4797
Supplies information on health organizations.

National Kidney Foundation
30 East 33rd Street
New York, NY 10016
(212) 889-2210
(800) 622-9010
Provides information and does research.

President's Council on Physical Fitness and Sports
701 Pennsylvania Avenue, N.W.
Suite 250
Washington, DC 20001
(202) 272-3421
Has information about physical education with a program especially suited for children.

Public Health Service
National AIDS Hotline
(800) 342-AIDS
Answers questions and gives referrals from databank; takes classroom calls with teacher guidance.

Runaway Hotline
(800) 231-6946
In Texas: (800) 392-3352

Provides crisis intervention line to runaways and their families.

United States Consumer Product Safety Commission
Washington, DC 20207
(800) 638-CPSC
Provides product recall information and general product safety information.

United States Department of Agriculture
Center for Nutrition Policy and Promotion
6505 Belcrest Road, Room 353
Hyattsville, MD 20782
(301) 436-5194
Publishes brochures providing current nutritional information.

TIPS FOR WRITING LETTERS TO ORGANIZATIONS

✓ If you are writing a letter as a class project, obtain permission to use school letterhead paper.

✓ If you are writing as an individual, use plain white paper but be sure to use your return address in your heading.

✓ Clearly and briefly state the reason for your letter and your specific request.

✓ If possible, type your letter. If you cannot type your letter, be sure your handwriting is easy to read.

✓ Be sure to check your spelling, grammar, and punctuation. Ask your teacher to check your letter before you send it.

✓ Check to be sure you have the correct address, including ZIP code, and the correct spelling of the name of the person to whom you are writing.

✓ Be sure to thank the person for his or her time and cooperation with you on your project.

The Language of Health

The language of health helps people communicate clearly when they talk about health topics. Here are some health words you can use when you talk with family, friends, and others about caring for your health.

A

acute, present for a short time, usually less than a month. **(B51)**

aerobic (air OH bihk) **exercise,** activity that causes deep breathing and a fast heart rate for at least 20 minutes. **(B32)**

AIDS, acquired immunodeficiency syndrome; caused by HIV, a virus that attacks blood cells and harms the body's ability to defend itself against other infections. **(B53)**

allergy, noncommunicable disorder in which a person has a bad reaction to a certain substance. **(B66)**

antibodies, chemicals in the body that help fight disease. **(B60)**

athlete's foot, fungal infection of the skin between the toes. **(B55)**

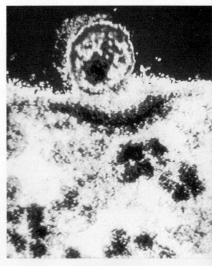

AIDS VIRUS

B

bacteria, very small, single-cell microbes, each of which is called a bacterium. **(B54)**

balanced diet, healthful amounts of foods from all five basic food groups; gives the body the nutrients it needs to stay healthy. **(B10)**

basic research, studies done in laboratories to discover scientific principles. **(B79)**

booster, vaccine that is given again to make a person's immunity to a disease stronger. **(B62)**

cancer, noncommunicable disease caused by cells growing out of control. **(B65)**

carbohydrate, nutrient in foods such as fruits, vegetables, breads, and cereals; should be the body's main source of energy. **(B3)**

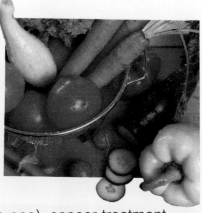

CARBOHYDRATES

chemotherapy (kee moh THEHR uh pee), cancer treatment in which the patient is given special drugs to fight cancer cells. **(B78)**

chronic, continuing for a long time, usually more than a month. **(B51)**

clinical research, study of better ways to treat patients. **(B79)**

communicable disease, illness that can be spread to a person from someone else or from something. **(B50)**

cool-down, activity done to allow the body to gradually return to normal after hard exercise. **(B35)**

diet, combination of foods that a person eats each day. **(B8)**

disease, breakdown in the way the body works. **(B48)**

disorder, noncommunicable health problem that may appear at birth or later in life. **(B64)**

endurance, ability to be active a long time without getting too tired to continue. **(B31)**

exercise, any activity that makes the body work hard. **(B24)**

TOE-TOUCH STRETCH

fat, nutrient that gives the body the greatest amount of energy. **(B3)**

fever, body temperature that is higher than normal. **(B54)**

fiber, substance in some plants that helps keep the body's digestive system healthy. **(B6)**

flexible, able to move the joints of the body easily and without tightness or pain. **(B33)**

fungi (FUHN jy), tiny plantlike organisms, some of which cause disease; *fungus* is the word for just one. **(B55)**

FUNGI

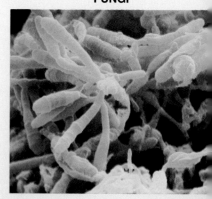

heart murmur, sound not usually made by a healthy heart. **(B65)**

immunity (ihm YOO nuht ee), ability of the body to defend itself from a certain disease. **(B59)**

infection, growth of disease microbes inside the body. **(B52)**

ingredients, materials used to make a food product. **(B15)**

injection, method of giving a person a vaccine or other medicine by inserting it through the skin with a needle; also called a shot. **(B61)**

microbe, living thing so small it can be seen only with a microscope. **(B52)**

MICROBES

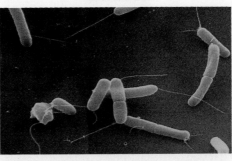

mineral, nutrient that does not give energy but is used by the body for growth and to do work. **(B5)**

muscle strength, ability of the body to apply force with its muscles. **(B29)**

noncommunicable disease, illness that cannot be spread from person to person. **(B50)**

nutrition, how the body uses food. **(B15)**

physical fitness, condition in which the body works the best that it can. **(B25)**

PINKEYE

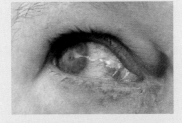

pinkeye, eye infection caused by bacteria. **(B56)**

posture, how a person holds his or her body. **(B30)**

prevent, to keep something from happening. **(B50)**

protein, nutrient that the body uses for the growth and repair of cells. **(B3)**

pulse, the push of blood through the blood vessels of the body with each heartbeat. **(B27)**

 R

relax, to become calm. **(B36)**

resistance, ability of the body to fight disease microbes by itself. **(B62)**

ringworm, skin infection caused by a fungus. **(B55)**

RINGWORM

 S

serving, for one food, the amount someone would be likely to eat during a meal. **(B11)**

stress, emotion that can make a person feel tense, as if the person were about to run or fight. **(B42)**

symptom, sign or feeling of a disease. **(B49)**

 T

thrush, fungus infection in the mouth. **(B55)**

treatment, care given a person who has a disease. **(B49)**

 V

vaccine (vak SEEN), substance that helps the body form immunity to a communicable disease. **(B61)**

viruses (VY ruhs uhz), very small microbes that can reproduce only inside a living cell. **(B53)**

vitamin, nutrient that does not give energy but helps cause a specific reaction in the body. **(B4)**

 W

warm-up, activity done to start harder exercise slowly. **(B33)**

Bold page numbers refer to illustrations.

National Center for Missing and Exploited Children, B99
National Commission Against Drunk Driving, C123
National Geographic Kids Network, A116, B94, C118
National Health Information Clearinghouse, B99
National Highway Traffic Safety Administration, C123
National Institute of Mental Health, A121
National Kidney Foundation, B99
National Mental Health Association, A121
National Safety Council, C123
Nature Conservancy, C115
Nearsightedness, A73, **A74**
    defined, A126
    eyeglasses for, A102
Needs, A10–A19
    change and, A14–A16, **A15**
    defined, A10, A126
    emotional, A12, A23, **A23**
    mental, A11, **A11**
    physical, A10–A11, **A10,** A22–A23, **A22**
    social, A12, **A12**
Negative intellectual trait, A5
Nerve cells, A52, A126
Nerves, A52–A54, **A53,** A126
    sensory, A54, **A55,** A128
    in skin, A57
    in teeth, **A65**
Nervous system, **A33,** A52–A57, **A53, A55, A128,** C25
Nicotine, C32, C33, **C33,** C34, C36, C126
911 telephone number, C47, C113, C126
Noise pollution, C86–C87, **C87,** C126
Noncommunicable disease, B50, B64–B67, B103
Nose, A34, A47, A54
Nuclear family, A21, **A21,** A126
Nurse, A98–A99, **A98, A99,** A127, C79, **C79**
Nutrients
    carbohydrates, B3, B10, B85, B101
    in circulatory system, A51, **A51**
    defined, A126
    fats, B3, B9, B10, B102
    fiber, B6–B7, **B7,** B102
    minerals, B5
    need for, A43, B2
    proteins, B3
    vitamins, B4, B104
    water, B6
Nutrition, B15, B103
Nutrition Nabber (software), B95

Nutritional deficiency, B5, B81, **B81**
Nuts, B9, B11, B85

Odors, A54, **A55,** A56, A57, B18, B19
Office of Substance Abuse Prevention, C123
Office of the Surgeon General, C123
O'Neill, Catherine, C117
On-line services, A116, B94, C118
Ophthalmoscope, A104, **A105**
Optometrist, A92
Oral cancer, C34, C127
Organ, A32, **A32,** A34, A127, **A127**
Organizations, directories of, A120–A121, B98–B99, C122–C123
Over-the-counter (OTC) medicines, C4–C6, C127, **C127**
Oxygen
    bacteria and, B54
    defined, A127
    exercise and, B77
    iron and, B5
    in respiratory system, A43, A47, A50

Packaging
    history of, C108–C110, **C109, C110**
    perils of, C110–C111
Pain control, A56
Parades, C60
Paramedic (EMT), C98
Parasite, B89
Paré, Ambroise, A105
Parents
    single, A21, **A21,** A128
    stepparents, A21
Pasta, B9, B11, B85
Pasta Factory (Machotka), B92
Pedestrian
    defined, C127
    safety of, C61–C62, **C61,** C104–C105
Pediatrician, A96–A97, **A96, A97**
Peer pressure
    acting against, C39–C40, **C39**
    alcohol use and, C27, C38
    defined, C127
    tobacco use and, C38–C41, **C39**

Permanent teeth, A63, A66, **A66,** A127, **A127**
Personal health log
    on anger, A13
    on care of teeth and gums, A71
    on community services, C81
    on disease prevention, B61
    on energy from foods, A31
    on exercise, B28, B35, B38
    on food choices, B9, B16
    on healthful habits, A87
    on illegal drugs, C17
    on making changes, A14
    on medicines, C6
    on rest, sleep, posture, and exercise, B38
    on safety, C62
    on self-concept, A9
    on smells, A56
    on specialness, A3
Personality, defined, A7, A127
Personality traits, A2
Pharmacist, C4, C100–C101, **C100, C101,** C127
Phosphorus, B5
Physical education connections
    cardiovascular fitness, A50
    exercise routine, B40
Physical education teacher, B76–B77, **B76, B77**
Physical fitness, B23, B24, B25–B45
    choices about, B39–B43
    defined, B103
    determining, B40
    endurance and, B31–B33, **B32, B33**
    exercise and, B23, B24–B35, **B26,** B39–B43, **B43**
    flexibility and, B33–B35, **B34, B35,** B102
    muscle strength and, B29–B31, **B29, B30**
    poster for, B31
    posture and, B28, B30–B31, **B31**
    rest and, B36–B38, **B36**
    sleep and, B36, B37, **B37,** B38
    wellness and, B31
Physical growth, A34–A37, **A35, A36, A37**
Physical needs
    of families, A11, A22–A23, **A22**
    of individuals, A10–A11, **A10**
Physical traits, A3–A4
Pinkeye, B50, B56, **B56,** B103
Pizzo, Philip A., B78–B79
Places to visit, A118–A119, B96–B97, C120–C121
Planning, for safety, C46–C50
Plaque, A67, **A67,** A68, A127